T0240565

Lecture Notes in Computer Science

Lecture Notes in Computer Science

Edited by G. Goos and J. Hartmanis

261

Johann Christoph Freytag

Translating Relational Queries into Iterative Programs

Springer-Verlag

Berlin Heidelberg New York London Paris Tokyo

Author

Johann Christoph Freytag
IBM Almaden Research Center K55/801
650 Harry Road, San Jose, CA 95120, USA

CR Subject Classification (1987): D.1.1, H.2.4, I.2.2

ISBN 3-540-18000-1 Springer-Verlag Berlin Heidelberg New York
ISBN 0-387-18000-1 Springer-Verlag New York Berlin Heidelberg

Library of Congress Cataloging-in-Publication Data. Freytag, Johann Christoph, 1954-. Trans-
lating relational queries into iterative programs. (Lecture notes in computer science; 261) Thesis
(Ph. D.)–Harvard University, 1985. Bibliography: p. 1. Relational data bases. 2. Electronic digital
computers–Programming. 3. Functional programming languages. I. Title. II. Series.
QA76.9.D3F75 1987 005.75'6 87-13054
ISBN 0-387-18000-1 (U.S.)

Printing and binding: Druckhaus Beltz, Hemsbach/Bergstr.
2145/3140-543210

Preface

This book is the published version of my thesis which I wrote as a Ph.D. student at Harvard University, Cambridge, MA, during 1985. Between 1982 and 1985, I spent three exciting years at this university developing the research ideas and results which are presented in this book. During this time, many people, directly and indirectly, contributed to the successful completion of this work.

I dedicate this book to my wife Susanne and my parents who both deserve my warmest thanks. Susannne's patience during my three years at Harvard made it possible for me to finish my dissertation successfully. In times of frustration her love and kindness have always been a source of strength and encouragement for me.

My parents' continuous care and guidance laid the foundations for this thesis. Their decision 25 years ago to escape from East Germany gave me the chance to become a student at Harvard.

At times, it seemed impossible to write this thesis. The infinite optimism of my advisor, Dr. Nathan Goodman, helped me overcome the difficulties finishing this dissertation. His trust in me and his far-sighted view guided me through my years at Harvard. He always challenged me and lead my research in new directions. His support and encouragement initiated my interest in functional programming and program transformation. I am grateful for his firm commitment to serve as my advisor for the last two years.

Prof. Philip A. Bernstein convinced me to return to Harvard as a Ph.D. student. Despite many changes and difficulties, he insured that I could continue my research at the Aiken Computation Laboratory successfully. His personality influenced my attitude as a researcher during my first year as a graduate student.

Special thanks also go to Prof. Harry R. Lewis and Prof. Mei Hsu who both invested their time in carefully reading my thesis. Their helpful comments improved the presentation of my ideas.

During the three years at Harvard I enjoyed the company of my fellow students. Doug Tygar deserves special thanks for his commitment to carefully read the first draft of my thesis despite the pressure I put on him. His critical comments improved this thesis in many ways. John Ramsdell introduced me to the mysterious world of functional programming. I am thankful for the many discussions and his patience in working with me. During the early stages of my research Dennis Shasha always had time for fruitful discussions which initiated many ideas. The discussions with Aviel Klausner clarified many thoughts, especially those in the first part of my thesis. Eleanor Sacks, Baiba Menke, and the rest of Aiken Lab's administrative staff provided the help and support which made everything much easier.

I am also grateful for a DAAD (Deutscher Akademischer Austauschdienst) fellowship which supported my studies at Harvard University for one year from 1979 to 1980. That time initiated my interest in becoming a Ph.D. student at this university.

Finally, I would like to thank the IBM Almaden Research Center and, in particular, my manager Dr. Laura Haas who provided me with the time and the resources to publish this thesis as a book.

This work was supported by the Office of Naval Research under grant ONR-N00014-83-K-0770.

Los Gatos, April 1987   Johann Christoph Freytag

Abstract

This book investigates the problem of translating set-oriented query specifications into iterative programs. The translation uses techniques of functional programming and program transformation.

The first part presents two algorithms which generate iterative programs from algebra-based query specifications. The first algorithm initially translates query specifications into recursive programs. Those are simplified by sets of transformation rules before the last step of the algorithm generates the final iterative form. The second algorithm uses a two level translation which generates iterative programs faster than the first algorithm. On the first level a small set of transformation rules performs structural simplification before the functional combination on the second level yields the final iterative form.

In the second part the same techniques are used to generate efficient programs for the evaluation of aggregate functions. One possible evaluation strategy is to sort the relation before applying the aggregate function, or better yet, to perform aggregation while sorting. Several transformation steps systematically generate these more efficient programs from separate specifications for the sort algorithm and the aggregate function.

Finally, the third part investigates the Lisp-dialect T as a possible implementation language for database systems.

Eigentlich weiß man nur,
wenn man wenig weiß;
mit dem Wissen wächst der Zweifel.

Die Wahlverwandtschaften
Johann Wolfgang Goethe (1749 - 1832)

Contents

List of Figures

List of Tables

Notation

$\mathcal{F}_{DB}$	Set of all database functions (DB functions).
$\mathcal{F}_I$	Set of form I DB functions.
$\mathcal{F}_{II}$	Set of form II DB functions.
$\mathcal{F}_{III}$	Set of form III DB functions.
L_{QEP}	Set of all well founded query evaluation plans (QEPs) which are composed of actions.
L_{DB}	Set of all database expressions (DB expressions) which are composed of DB functions.
L_{map}	Set of all well founded map expressions.
L_λ	Set of all λ-expressions.
Σ	Mapping from DB expressions to map expressions.
Ω	Mapping from map expressions to λ-expressions.
$(\mathcal{T}_P, \mathcal{R}_P)$	Transformation system for recursive functions.
$(\mathcal{T}_P, \mathcal{R}_U)$	Transformation system for union functions.
$(\mathcal{T}_{map}, \mathcal{R}_{map})$	Transformation system for map expressions.
$(\mathcal{T}_\lambda, \mathcal{R}_\lambda)$	Transformation system for lambda expressions.
$B(f_1)$	function body of function f_1.

$s(f_1, f_2, i)$	Substitution of function expression calling f_2 as the ith parameter in the function expression calling f_1.
$S(f_1, f_2, i)$	Substitution of the body of function f_2 for the ith parameter into the body of function f_1.
$\mathcal{TR}_R$	Recursion based transformation algorithm.
$\mathcal{ID}$	Transformation algorithm to produce the ideal form which is a transformation step in algorithm $\mathcal{TR}_R$.
$\mathcal{RI}$	Transformation step in algorithm $\mathcal{TR}_R$ to generate iterative programs from ideal forms.
$\mathcal{UF}$	Unfolding step in transformation algorithm $\mathcal{ID}$.
$\mathcal{FL}$	Folding step in transformation algorithm $\mathcal{ID}$.
$\mathcal{SIM}$	Simplification step in transformation algorithm $\mathcal{ID}$ using transformation system $(\mathcal{T}_P, \mathcal{R}_P)$.
$\mathcal{UN}$	Union step in transformation algorithm $\mathcal{ID}$ using transformation system $(\mathcal{T}_P, \mathcal{R}_U)$.
$\mathcal{TR}_{map}$	Transformation algorithm based on map expressions and λ-expressions.
$\mathcal{T}_{map}$	Transformation step for map expressions in algorithm $\mathcal{TR}_{map}$.
$\mathcal{ML}$	Transformation step for λ-expressions in algorithm $\mathcal{TR}_{map}$.
$\mathcal{TR}_\lambda$	Simplification step for λ-expressions in algorithm $\mathcal{ML}$ using transformation system $(\mathcal{T}_\lambda, \mathcal{R}_\lambda)$.
$\mathcal{A}(t, r)$	Applying rule r exhaustively to term t.
$\mathcal{AP}(t_1, t_2)$	Applying lambda expression t_2 to lambda expression t_1.

Chapter 1

Introduction

1.1 Statement of Problem

A *database* models some enterprise by a set of data structures abstracting relevant facts of that enterprise. With today's computer technology data are frequently stored and accessed by a *database system* (dbs). Such a system provides a uniform interface for the definition of internal structures to store, modify, and access data. Operations are expressed by a *query language*: the user defines requests by queries which the database system then executes to produce the desired result.

In a *relational database system* [Cod70] [Ull82], queries are expressed in a data independent manner: the user formulates a request without knowing anything about the internal representation of the data accessed. Instead (s)he refers to *relations* as their external representation. A relation consists of *tuples*, or *records*, which hide internal details of representation from the user. A query describes only conditions that the final response to the request must satisfy. It does not determine the strategy for computing the response. Therefore, the database system is responsible for developing an evaluation strategy which computes the desired result efficiently. The component which decides on the best evaluation strategy is called the *query optimizer*.

Using the information about the internal data representation, the query optimizer generates a *query evaluation plan* (QEP) for a submitted user query. In this thesis we assume that a query evaluation plan describes the query computation in terms of set-oriented operations [RR82]. Before it can be executed, a query evaluation plan must be translated into a program which operates on

1

tuples as its basic objects. We call the problem of generating this program from a QEP the *translation problem for relational queries*. The next section describes the problem in more detail and outlines solutions which are currently used. Their disadvantages lead to the different approach taken in this thesis.

Our approach to the translation problem is based on techniques and results of *functional programming* and *program transformation* [BD77]. Functional programming formalism helps us to formulate simple algebraic rules. Those rules manipulate programs in their functional form to derive efficient iterative programs from initial query plans. Some important aspects of functional programming and program transformation are discussed in the final section of this chapter.

This thesis is divided into seven chapters. Chapter 2 describes the source and the target level of the translation and outlines important concepts of *term rewriting systems* [Hue80]. Chapters 3 and 4 develop two different, but closely related algorithms for the translation of algebra based QEPs into iterative programs. The first algorithm gives an elegant solution to the translation problem. However its inefficiency motivated the design of the second one, which advances more quickly towards the final iterative program. For both algorithms we discuss possible extensions to generate programs for evaluating several queries simultaneously.

Both algorithms are restricted to the translation of algebra based QEPs. Chapter 5 extends the transformational approach to the evaluation of *aggregate functions*. We suggest transformation strategies which derive efficient iterative programs from modular specifications for their computation.

The concepts developed in Chapters 2 to 5 naturally raise the question of whether functional languages are appropriate for the implementation of database systems. Chapter 6 investigates the Lisp dialect T as a possible implementation language and implementation environment [RA82] [RAM83]. We analyze T's expressiveness and compare it in execution speed with the programming language C [KR78] to evaluate its performance behavior.

Finally, Chapter 7 summarizes the contributions of this thesis and briefly outlines open problems which are closely related to the translation problem of relational queries. Encouraged by our results, we suggest applying the techniques and ideas of functional programming and program transformation to more problems in the area of database systems.

1.2 Query Optimization and Evaluation

In a relational database system we distinguish two major components: the *logical database processor* (LDBP) and the *physical database processor* (PDBP). The LDBP translates a user-submitted query into an internal representation and optimizes it to guarantee efficient execution. The *query optimizer*, a subcomponent of the LDBP, decides on the best evaluation strategy for a user-submitted query. Information about the internal representation of the data accessed by the query and the evaluation strategies available for each operator in the query influence the generation of a *query evaluation plan* (QEP). For instance, the existence of indices or information about the physical order of elements may influence the optimizer's choice of either an index-join or a merge-join as the optimal evaluation strategy of a join operation. [RR82] describes an architecture for a query optimizer which successively derives a more detailed representation for a given query before constructing the final QEP. This layered approach facilitates a possible extension of an optimizer to allow additional query operators and to include new evaluation strategies. *Set-oriented operators* describe the final output of the optimizer. Their use permits changes to the implementation of the underlying PDBP without affecting the implementation of the query optimizer.

After the optimizer has generated its final QEP, the PDBP must evaluate the QEP against the database to compute the requested result. The PDBP has to satisfy two conflicting requirements: On the one hand, its interface should be set-oriented thus allowing the immediate evaluation of QEPs; on the other hand, it must be amenable to an efficient execution. To ensure the latter many database systems implement a PDBP whose basic operations manipulate *tuples*, or *records*. To execute QEPs, the database systems then provide a set of procedures which *independently* implement the various set-oriented operators permitted in QEPs. These procedures access data using tuple-oriented operations by the PDBP. For example, Lorie et al. suggest a set-oriented access specification language ASL which precisely describes all valid operators for QEPs in SYSTEM R [LB79].

Those are implemented as parameterized procedures in terms of operations on the Relational Storage System (RSS), the PDBP in SYSTEM R [A*76]. [BF82] defines a similar system that takes advantage of *lazy evaluation* [HM76] [FW76], which retains intermediate results between operators as small as one tuple. All these systems give an *interpretive* solution to the translation problem of relational queries. The solution described in this thesis *transforms*, or *compiles*, the set-oriented QEPs into *iterative programs* which are then executable on the tuple-oriented interface of the PDBP. The transformational approach is a natural solution to the translation problem and eliminates much of the overhead in the interpretive approach.

Relational database systems usually provide two modes for executing user queries. In the first mode, each time the user submits a query the database system optimizes it, thereby producing a QEP, and executes the QEP against the database. So if same query or set of queries are submitted frequently, the same QEP is repeatedly created unnecessarily.[1] To eliminate the redundant creation of the QEP, the database system offers a second mode in which it internally stores the QEP, that it generates when it executes the query the first time. If the user resubmits the query, the database system retrieves the corresponding QEP and immediately executes it instead of repeating its generation. A further improvement in execution time is possible by replacing the QEP by a program that is directly executable on the PDBP. SYSTEM R implements the first improvement; QEPs are translated into assembler programs, called access modules, which coordinate the calls to the different ASL procedures.

This thesis describes a solution to the translation problem which includes both improvements outlined above. We develop algorithms that translate QEPs into programs directly executable on the PDBP. C [KR78] or PASCAL [JW75], extended by operations of the PDBP, are possible target languages of our translation. Existing compilers for these languages can then translate the generated programs into machine executable ones.

Our two-level translation approach has several advantages over the solution of SYSTEM R. First and most important, the generation of iterative

---

[1] If the internal structure of the database has not changed.

programs from modular specifications *minimizes the amount of overhead during execution*. Procedure calls and repeated evaluation of the same functions are eliminated. The compiler may further optimize the iterative programs during the compilation into machine language. Second, the generation of programs in higher level languages guarantees a certain degree of *machine independence*: The creation of these programs does not require any knowledge of a particular machine environment. Switching compilers achieves portability onto different machines. Third, the separation into two independent steps *simplifies* the translation problem. High level programming constructs easily express QEPs without considering other aspects during the generation of programs in the target language. Additionally, the suggested translation avoids duplicating tasks that compilers already perform. We assume that they carry out standard program optimization and optimization for a particular machine environment.

We present our programs in a Lisp-like notation which describes the programs independently of specific language structures. Our choice frees us from many details which are necessary for a complete specification, but unimportant for the development of the different transformation algorithms. Our choice also reflects the notation used throughout this thesis to describe the different transformations in a uniform way. However, the programs we generate may easily be translated into programs using procedural programming languages.

1.3 Functional Programming and Program Transformation

This section reviews some important aspects of *functional programming* and *program transformation*. Many ideas and results of these two areas influenced, shaped and contributed to our solutions of the query translation problem in this thesis.

Generally speaking, program transformation promises to provide a comprehensive solution to the problem of producing programs which try to meet several incompatible goals simultaneously: On one hand, programs should be correct and clearly structured, thus allowing easy modification. On the other hand, one expects them to be executed efficiently. Using languages like C or

5

PASCAL for the implementation of programs one is immediately forced to consider aspects of efficiency which are often unrelated to their correctness, natural structure and clarity.

For this reason, the transformational approach tries to separate these two concerns by dividing the programming task into two steps: The first step concentrates on producing of programs that are written as clearly and understandably as possible without considering efficiency issues. If initially the question of efficiency is completely ignored, the resulting programs might be written very comprehensibly, but be highly inefficient or even unexecutable. The second step successively transforms programs into more efficient ones — possibly for a particular machine environment — using methods which preserve the meaning of the original program. The kind of improvements which are necessary during the second step must go beyond the ones achievable by the optimization phase of conventional compilers.

In many ways, these intentions guided the design of query languages for relational database systems such as QUEL [SW*76] or SQL [A*76]. Both languages permit the user to express his or her request in a clear and understandable form that describes properties of the requested result without considering an efficient execution. As we discussed in the previous section, the database system has to find an efficient execution strategy. The query optimizer produces a QEP which determines all steps of an evaluation. However, the QEP still needs further refinement to guarantee an efficient execution on conventional computer systems.

Since program transformations require significant manipulations, an applicative or functional language, such as LISP is used as an especially convenient notation for writing programs. Turner observes out that "programs written in these languages can be manipulated using the ordinary rules of algebra rather than the very complex rules needed when manipulating programs written in languages such as PASCAL or ALGOL" [Tur80].

Many early transformation methods considered the manipulation of recursively defined programs or programs defined by recursive equations [DB76]. As Burstall and Darlington state, "the recursive form seems well adapted to manipulation, much more than the usual Algol-style form of programs..." [BD77]. Much research has focused on transformation schemes that replace recursion by itera-

6

tion. Cohen gives a comprehensive overview of various approaches and solutions which have been developed for different types of recursions [Coh80]. Burstall and Darlington developed a set of transformation schemes for removal of recursion together with a systematic approach for the manipulation of recursive programs [DB76] [BD77]. They introduce transformation steps such as *unfolding, folding, abstraction,* and *the application of simplification rules.* Using these steps, they successfully implemented a semi-automatic transformation system. Their work influenced the design of new applicative languages, such as HOPE [BMS80].

John Backus' Turing award lecture introduced a new style of programming using the FP language [Bac78]. As Williams explains, "The FP style of functional programming differs from the lambda (i.e. recursive) style in that the emphasis in the former is on the application of functionals (i.e. combining forms) to functions, whereas the emphasis in the latter is on the application of functions to objects to produce new objects" [Wil82]. Much of the current research in functional programming and program transformation has centered around this new approach [Bir84] [Col84] [Bel84]. Many of the proposed transformations need user guidance; only a few systems perform transformation without user intervention [Bel84].

The different transformation systems developed in this thesis to solve the query translation problem reflect the two directions in program transformation. Chapter 3 develops a translation algorithm which exclusively relies on the definition of recursive programs and their transformation by unfolding, folding, and rule driven simplification. The final output is an iterative program expressed in a Lisp-like notation. Unfortunately, long transformations often result, mainly due to very small changes in each step of the simplification phase and difficulties during the folding phase. This encouraged us to develop a new transformation system based on ideas of Backus' FP language. The transformation, described in Chapter 4, leads to the final program form much faster.

The translation of programs for the computation of aggregate functions in Chapter 5 is best described by a combination of both approaches. First, the manipulation of control structures relies on the concepts and ideas of the FP language. The second step combines initially independent recursive programs to new recursive programs which then lead to an iterative program form. The

7

second part of the transformation includes an abstraction step that requires some user guidance to obtain the desired program form.

The description of the different transformation systems in all three chapters suggests an implementation using an applicative language. We investigate the Lisp dialect T as a possible implementation environment for database systems [RAM83] [RA82]. In Chapter 6 we compare the execution speed of two PDBPs implemented in languages T and C [KR78]. Measured results indicate that T is far too slow to serve as a realistic implementation environment for database systems.

Example 1

To demonstrate different transformations we shall use the following two relations containing data of employees at a university.

```
EMP (Emp#, Name, Salary, Dept, Status)
PAPERS (Emp#, Title, Year)
```

Each tuple in relation EMP describes an employee by his or her employee number, name, salary, department, and status. Relation PAPERS stores the employees who have written papers, recording the title and the year of the publication. We assume that relation EMP *has an index* on attribute Status called ISTAT. □

Chapter 2

Data Models and Rewriting Systems

This chapter introduces the two concepts which together form the common base for this thesis; they are essential for the solutions presented in the following chapters. First, we describe *the data models* and their operations for QEPs and for the PDBP which form the *source and the target level* of the translation. Additionally, we introduce a language which is powerful enough to express iterative programs executable on the PDBP. Second, we describe *term rewriting systems* which transform expressions of the language using rules.

As the final output of the query optimizer, a QEP determines the major computational steps, or *actions*, for the evaluation of a query. We assume that these actions are specified by set-oriented operations [RR82], a rather high-level description of the intended computation. To express QEPs formally, we define a data model together with a set of valid operators. This set is sufficiently large enough to express important aspects of the translation process. Our choice of operators does not impose any serious limitations on our approach. Other operators can be easily added to the existing ones to obtain a more complete set for "real world" database systems.

For the PDBP we consider a small, but sufficient, set of tuple-oriented operators describing the most important operational aspects of PDBPs. Together with the simple language which we introduce, the defined operator set is sufficiently complete for the implementation of actions in QEPs on the PDBP.

Several steps of the transformation algorithm described in the following chapters are based on sets of rules that successively rewrite programs and generate new ones. These *term rewriting systems*, or *tree replacement systems*, have been studied extensively by several researchers [Hue80] [Ros73]. Generally, a term rewriting system is a model of computation. It describes, for example, the manipulation of formulas used in various applications, such as program optimization [ASU72], automatic theorem proving, or partial evaluation [B*76]. The final section reviews the important aspects and results of term rewriting systems.

2.1 Data Models and their Operations

This section defines in detail the data models and operations used for the specification of QEPs and for the PDBP. The models form the source and the target level of the translation. The former is based on the standard index file organization, such as used by [A*76] or [RR82]. We use *tables* as an abstract data structure to separate the target level from details of the data model used for a particular PDBP. A table is a collection of similarly structured *tuples*, or *records*, which are stored on secondary memory. Each tuple consists of a sequence of *attributes*, or *fields*, whose contents is accessed by *attribute names* or *field names*. The attribute names and number of attributes are the same for all tuples in the same table. Tables storing user provided data are called *data tables*. Each *data tuple* is uniquely identified by a *tuple identifier* (TID), which is a logical pointer [A*76]. In addition to data tables, the model includes *access tables*, or *indices*, which store *access tuples* of the form *<value(s), TID>*. These tables support fast access to individual tuples in data tables.

The set of operators consists of the following two subsets: operators in the first subset, called *source operators*, provide access to tables in the database or to parts of tables. They return either a set of tuples or access to a table. Operators in the second group, called *set operators*, transform sets of tuples into sets of tuples. Sets of tuples differ from tables in that we leave unspecified if they reside in main memory or on secondary memory. This aspect will become irrelevant for the performed transformations. We define both groups of operators as follows:

(SCAN table)

is a source operator that accesses a table and returns the *set of all its tuples*. Our definition only determines the source and leaves the destination unspecified.[1]

(*SEARCH pred? access_table*)

is a source operator that returns a table with all the tuples satisfying the predicate *pred?*. The operator *SCAN* may then retrieve the tuples in the restricted access table. The predicate is a boolean formula over terms of the form $(t_1 \; cop \; t_2)$, where *cop* represents any comparison operator, and t_1 and t_2 refer to constants or attribute names of the stored tuples. Its precise format is unimportant for the translation.

(*GET data_table set_of_access_tuples*)

is a set operator that retrieves all corresponding tuples in the specified data table by TIDs given the input set of access tuples.

(*FILTER pred? set_of_tuples*)

is a set operator that returns the subset of those tuples satisfying the predicate *pred?*. The predicate *pred?* has the same form as in the *SEARCH* operator.

(*PROJECT project_list set_of_tuples*)

is a set operator that projects a set of tuples onto the specified attributes of the projection list.

(*LJOIN join? set_1 set_2*)

is a set operator that defines a *loop join* [Ull82]. Each tuple in the first set is matched with every tuple in the second set to test the join predicate *join?*. If the test evaluates to *true* for two tuples their concatenation is added to the output set.

This set of operators forms the basis for the definition of QEPs. A QEP is said to be *well formed* if it is either a source operator accessing a data or access table, or a set operator whose input set is defined by a well formed QEP.

---

[1][RR82] uses the same operator to move an entire table from a source to a destination location.

We assume that all other parameters to the operators are correctly provided according to the above definitions.

Example 2

We use the database introduced in example 1 on page 8 to evaluate the following query:

Find the names of all professors who published papers after 1980.

The following QEP expresses one possible evaluation strategy for this query. The query optimizer may have decided that it performs the evaluation best for the submitted query.

$(PROJECT$ (Name)
$\qquad (LJOIN$ (Emp# = Emp#)
$\qquad\qquad (GET$ EMP
$\qquad\qquad\qquad (SCAN$ $(SEARCH$ (Status $= Prof$) ISTAT)))
$\qquad\qquad (FILTER$ (Year > 1980) $(SCAN$ PAPERS))))

$\qquad$ □

The current set does not include operators to create new tables or to store tuples in tables. Furthermore, none of the operators create intermediate results during their computation. That is, sets of tuples are not stored temporarily in tables before the final set of tuples is computed. The form of programs generated by the transformation algorithm will reflect this restriction. Clearly, there exist important operators, such as the sort operator, which require the creation of tables to store intermediate results. However, the current set of operators can easily be extended to cope with intermediate results: we include an additional operator to create new tables and extend QEPs to *query programs* (QPs), i. e. straight line sequences of QEPs. QPs may express any evaluation requiring intermediate results: the query is divided into parts; each part is evaluated by some QEP which stores its intermediate result in a newly created table.

While the data model for QEPs performs operations on sets of tuples and tables, the PDBP operates on *individual tuples*. Abstracting from particular implementations, we introduce the notion of *streams* [FW76]. Streams are sequences of tuples which were used by [FW76] in the context of lazy evaluation. In any stream only the first element is computed. The rest of the stream is evaluated only if needed. In our context the word connotes images of tuples *streaming through* the different operators. We define a generic set of operators that manipulate streams while hiding details of a specific PDBP. This approach treats the access to tables and sets of tuples in a uniform way. We define the following five operators which access, create, and test streams:

(*first stream*)	:	returns the first element in the *stream*.
(*rest stream*)	:	returns a new stream by removing the first element in *stream*.
empty	:	is the empty stream.
(*out ele stream*)	:	creates a new stream whose first element is *ele* followed by all elements in *stream*.
(*empty? stream*)	:	evaluates to true if *stream* is empty and to false if *stream* is an expression of the form (*out ele str*).

For completeness two more operators are necessary to manipulate data and access tables:

(*get_tuple data_table access_tuple*) : given an *access_tuple* the operator returns a tuple from the *data_table* according to the TID value of the access tuple.

(*search pred? access_table*) : returns a table containing all tuples which satisfy the provided predicate *pred?*. This operator directly implements action *SEARCH* for QEPs without specifying further details of its implementation.

According to the above definitions for QEPs and the PDBP, the sets of valid operators O_{QEP} and O_{PDBP} for both levels are:

O_{QEP} = { $SCAN, SEARCH, GET, FILTER, PROJECT, LJOIN$ }

O_{PDBP} = { $first, rest, empty?, *empty*, out, get\_tuple, search$ }

13

2.2 The Target Language

While actions in QEPs completely specify the source language, a target language has to be defined to completely express the programs resulting from the translation. For this purpose we propose a small functional language in a Lisp-like notation which is well suited for formal manipulation. We will describe the target language informally. The language is based on *expressions*. An expression is either a *variable*, a *function expression* or a *conditional expression*. A function expression has the form $(f_1 \; t_1 \ldots t_n)$ where f_1 is a function symbol and t_i, $i = 1, \ldots, n$, are expressions, called actual parameters. A conditional expression has the form $(if \; t_1 \; t_2 \; t_3)$, where t_1, t_2 and t_3 are expressions. If t_1 evaluates to *true*, then the value of t_2 is the value of the expression, otherwise it is the value of t_3. When t_3 is superfluous we use the form $(if \; t_1 \; t_2)$.

In addition to expressions, we introduce the *definitions of functions* by the equation $(f_1 \; x_1 \ldots x_n) \;=\; t_1$ where f_1 is a function symbol, the x_i are formal parameters, and t_1 is an expression built from function symbols, possibly including f_1 and variables x_i. $(f_1 \; x_1 \ldots x_n)$ is called the *function header* of f_1 with t_1 as its *function body* $B(f_1)$. $F(B(f_1))$ denotes the set of all functions called in the body of f_1. If f_1 is called in a function expression, then its value is determined by substituting $B(f_1)$ for the expression and replacing the formal parameters by the actual ones.

Functions and expressions are sufficient for most steps in the translation process. However, to express iterative programs we extend the language by an *assignment statement* and a *loop statement*. Generally, these statements do not occur in function definitions; again they are used only in the final output of the transformation. An assignment statement is of the form $(set \; x \; t_1)$ where x is a variable and t_1 is an expression. The loop statement has the form $(do \; (x \; t_1 \; t_2) \; t_3 \; t_4)$ with x as a variable, t_1, t_2, t_3 as expressions, and t_4 is an assignment statement or an expression. The semantics of the loop statement can be described best by the PASCAL-like program:

$$x \;:=\; t_1; \; \text{WHILE } t_3 \text{ DO BEGIN } t_4 \;;\; x \;:=\; t_2; \text{ END};$$

14

2.3 Term Rewriting Systems

In this section we briefly introduce the theory of *term rewriting systems* as it is presented in [Hue80]. We give some basic definitions necessary to derive his *theorem of confluence*. Confluence guarantees that the final result of rule based transformation is independent of the application order of the rules. This property is often called the *Church-Rosser* property, or CR for short.

Let $\mathcal{V}$ be a set of variables, denoted by t_1, t_2,... and $\mathcal{F}$ be a finite set of function symbols, denoted by f_1, f_2,..., f_m, such that $\mathcal{V} \cap \mathcal{F} = \emptyset$. Let $\mathcal{N}$ be the natural numbers $0, 1, \ldots$. For each function $f \in \mathcal{F}$ we define its *arity* $a(f) \in \mathcal{N}$ as the number of variables in the function definition. Let $\mathcal{F}_n = \{f : a(f) = n\}$ denote the functions in $\mathcal{F}$ of arity n. The *set of terms* $\mathcal{T}$ over $\mathcal{F}$ and $\mathcal{V}$ is defined as follows:

- each variable $t \in \mathcal{V}$ is a term

- $(f\ t_1 \ldots t_n)$ is a term if $f \in \mathcal{F}_n$, and $t_1, \ldots, t_n$ are terms.

- $(z\ t_1 \ldots t_n)$ is a term if $t_1, \ldots, t_n$ are terms and z is a variable representing any function $f \in \mathcal{F}_n$.

Let $\mathcal{T}(t) = \{t\} \cup \bigcup_{i=1}^{n} \mathcal{T}(t_i)$ denote the set of subterms in $t = (f\ t_1 \ldots t_n)$, and let $V(t)$ represent the set of all variables occurring in t. A *substitution* is defined as a mapping σ from variables to terms, i. e. from $\mathcal{V}$ to $\mathcal{T}$. We say that $t_2 \in \mathcal{T}$ is *obtained* from $t_1 \in \mathcal{T}$ if there exists a mapping σ for all variables $x_i \in V(t_1)$ such that $t_2 = \sigma(t_1)$. If σ maps variables into variables then then we say that t_1 and t_2 are *congruent*, and write $t_1 \sim t_2$. Instead of writing $\sigma(t)$ where $\sigma(x_i) = t_i$, $i = 1 \ldots n$, we often prefer the notation $t\,[x_1\,/\,t_1 \ldots x_n\,/\,t_n]$.

A term rewriting system, or tree replacement system [Ros73], is a pair $(\mathcal{T},\ \mathcal{R})$ where $\mathcal{T}$ is a (possibly infinite) set of terms and $\mathcal{R}$ a (possibly infinite) set of pairs $(a,\ b)$, called *rules* with $(a, b) \in \mathcal{T}$ and $V(b) \subseteq V(a)$. For convenience we denote rules by $(a \longrightarrow b)$ instead of (a, b). A rule $r = (a \longrightarrow b)$ is *applicable* to term $t \in \mathcal{T}$ if there exist a subterm t_1 in t such that t_1 can be obtained from a.

15

Let t_1 be an expression and let $r = (a \longrightarrow b)$ be a rule in $\mathcal{R}$ which is applicable to t_1. Then there exists a subterm t_3 in t_1 and a mapping σ such that $t_3 = \sigma(a)$. If $\sigma(b)$ replaces t_3 in t_1 resulting in expression t_2 then we say term t_1 *reduces* to term t_2. Extending the bracket notation to terms we write $t_2 = t_1 [t_3 / \sigma(b)]$ where $t_3 = \sigma(a)$.

More general, term t *derives* term t' using $\mathcal{R}$ if there exists a sequence $\mathcal{D} = (t_0, t_1, \ldots, t_n)$ of terms such that $t_0 = t$, $t_n = t'$ and each t_i reduces to t_{i+1} by some rule in $\mathcal{R}$. $\mathcal{D}$ is called *derivation sequence* of *length* n; the corresponding sequence of rules yielding the derivation sequence is called *rule sequence*. Any derivation of t' from t is denoted by $t \overset{*}{\longrightarrow} t'$; in case of a 1-step derivation we write $t \longrightarrow t'$. Using derivations we define a partial order $\succ$:

$$t_1 \succ t_2 \text{ iff } t_1 \overset{*}{\longrightarrow} t_2$$

The partial order $\succ$ can be completed with a maximum element to form a complete lattice [Hue80]. The *upper bound predicate ub* and *lower bound predicate lb* for two terms are defined by:

- $ub(t_1, t_2) : \exists t_3 : t_3 \overset{*}{\longrightarrow} t_1$ and $t_3 \overset{*}{\longrightarrow} t_2$ with $t_1, t_2, t_3 \in \mathcal{T}$

- $lb(t_1, t_2) : \exists t_3 : t_1 \overset{*}{\longrightarrow} t_3$ and $t_2 \overset{*}{\longrightarrow} t_3$ with $t_1, t_2, t_3 \in \mathcal{T}$

If $ub(t_1, t_2)$ is true then $t = LUB(t_1, t_2)$ denotes the least of such elements t_3.

We now introduce *critical pairs* in a term rewriting system. Informally, two rules r_1, r_2 whose left hand sides can be, at least partially, matched, derive a pair of new expressions, called a critical pair, which describes the two "directions" a derivation takes using these two rules. We may use the *superposition algorithm* by Knuth and Bendix for the computation of critical pairs [KB70]. More formally, let $(\mathcal{T}, \mathcal{R})$ be a term rewriting system and $r_1 = (a_1 \longrightarrow b_1)$ and $r_2 = (a_2 \longrightarrow b_2)$ be rules in $\mathcal{R}$. Let a_1 contain a subterm t_1, such that $t_2 = LUB(t_1, a_2)$ with $t_2 = \sigma_1(t_1)$, $t_2 = \sigma_2(a_2)$ assuming that $V(t_2) \cap V(a_2) = \emptyset$. We say that the *superposition of r_2 on r_1 at t_1* determines the *critical pair* (t', t'') with $t' = \sigma_1(a_1) [\sigma_1(t_1), / \sigma_2(b_2)]$ and $t'' = \sigma_1(b_1)$.

$\mathcal{R}$ may not have any critical pairs induced by its rules. On the other hand there may exist more than one critical pair for any two rules r_1, r_2 in $\mathcal{R}$.

Example: Let

$$r_1 = ((z\ (f_1\ t_1'\ t_2'\ t_3')) \longrightarrow (f_1\ t_1'\ (z\ t_2')\ (z\ t_3')));$$
$$r_2 = ((f_1\ (f_1\ t_1\ t_2\ t_3)\ t_4\ t_5) \longrightarrow (f_1\ t_1\ (f_1\ t_2\ t_4\ t_5)\ (f_1\ t_3\ t_4\ t_5)))$$

where $f_1, f_2 \in \mathcal{F}$, $t_i, t_i' \in \mathcal{V}$, $z \in \mathcal{V}$ as a function variable. The superposition of r_2 on r_1 determines the critical pair (t', t'') with

$$t' = (z\ (f_1\ t_1\ (f_1\ t_2\ t_4\ t_5)\ (f_1\ t_3\ t_4\ t_5)))$$
$$t'' = (f_1\ (f_1\ t_1\ t_2\ t_3)\ (z\ t_4)\ (z\ t_5))$$

Note that there exists another critical pair for r_2 by superposing the rule on itself. □

In the following we define some properties of term rewriting systems which are important in our context. We say that $(\mathcal{T}, \mathcal{R})$ is *noetherian* if for each $t \in \mathcal{T}$ there does not exist an infinite derivation using $\mathcal{R}$; the system is *bounded* if for each term $t \in \mathcal{T}$ there exists a $n \in \mathcal{N}$ such that any derivation under $\mathcal{R}$ beginning with t is shorter than n. If $\mathcal{R}$ is finite, then $(\mathcal{T}, \mathcal{R})$ is bounded iff $(\mathcal{T}, \mathcal{R})$ is noetherian. A term $t \in \mathcal{T}$ which cannot be reduced by any rule in $\mathcal{R}$ is called *minimal*, or *irreducible*. If $t \in \mathcal{T}$ derives t' which is minimal, then t' is called a *normal form* of t.

Given a term rewriting system $(\mathcal{T}, \mathcal{R})$ we say that $(\mathcal{T}, \mathcal{R})$ is *confluent* iff $\forall t_1, t_2 \in \mathcal{T} : ub(t_1, t_2) \Rightarrow lb(t_1, t_2)$, that is if t_1 and t_2 share a common term t' such that t' derives t_1 and t_2, then there exists a term t'' such that t_1 derives t'' and t_2 derives t''. If $(\mathcal{T}, \mathcal{R})$ is confluent and noetherian then it *converges*.

Lemma 2.1 [Hue80] *If $(\mathcal{T}, \mathcal{R})$ is confluent then the normal form of any term $t_1 \in \mathcal{T}$, if it exists, is unique.*

If $(\mathcal{T}, \mathcal{R})$ is also noetherian, a normal form does exist for any term t, and by the previous lemma it is unique.

Lemma 2.2 [Hue80] *If $(\mathcal{T}, \mathcal{R})$ is confluent then the following property holds:*

$$\forall t_1, t_2 : t_1 \overset{*}{\longleftrightarrow} t_2 \Longleftrightarrow lb(t_1, t_2)$$

where $t_1 \overset{*}{\longleftrightarrow} t_2$ is the symmetric transitive closure induced by $\mathcal{R}$. This property is often called the Church-Rosser property (CR property).

Both lemmas show the importance of confluence for term rewriting systems. [Hue80] provides a test of confluence for noetherian term rewriting systems; we shall freely use his test in the following chapters:

Theorem 2.1 [Hue80] *Let (T, R) be a noetherian term rewriting system; it is confluent iff for every critical pair (t_1, t_2) induced by rules in R we have $\hat{t}_1 = \hat{t}_2$ where $\hat{t}_i$ denotes the normal form of t_i.*

If R is finite then the number of critical pairs is finite. Since (T, R) is noetherian the computation of both unique normal forms by an arbitrary derivation is guaranteed to terminate.

Chapter 3

A Transformation System based on Recursive Programs

As a first solution to the translation problem of relational queries, this chapter develops a transformation algorithm based on the *manipulation of recursive programs*. The first section defines recursive programs, or functions, for each action in a QEP. Each function correctly implements the corresponding action.

The following sections then describe the four major steps of the transformation algorithm: The first step, called *unfolding*, or *substitution*, replaces an action by its corresponding recursive function. During the second step, a set of transformation rules *simplifies* the initial program without changing its intended meaning. The simplification step leads to a *canonical form* of the program. The third step, *folding*, further reduces the program generated so far. This step is the inverse of unfolding. Using the recursive function form produced by the third step, the final step replaces recursion by iteration.

The complete transformation algorithm is presented in Section 3.5. The final section of this chapter outlines a *user guided* transformation using recursive definitions to further improve programs derived from QEPs.

3.1 DB Functions and DB Expressions

To perform the first step of the transformation we define programs, called *DB functions*, for each valid action of a QEP. A combination of DB functions is called *DB expression*. While actions are denoted by *capital letters*, DB functions

19

will be denoted by *lower case letters*. They are defined by expressions of the target language introduced in Section 2.3. Each DB function calls only itself, functions of the PDBP, other DB functions, and possibly additional functions which are denoted by `pred?`, `join?`, and `prj`. Functions `pred?`, `join?`, and `prj` *implement* the predicates used as the first parameter to actions *FILTER* and *LJOIN*, and the projection list for action *PROJECT*, respectively. We denote the arguments to actions by *capital letters*, i.e. *PRED?*, *JOIN?*, and *PRJ*, and the functions implementing them by *lower case letters*, i.e. `pred?`, `join?`, and `prj`. For the transformation developed in the following sections it is unimportant how these functions implement the predicates and the projection list. For our purposes it is sufficient to denote the implementing functions by names in lower case letters. For the implementation of *LJOIN* we also introduce the function *conc* to concatenate two tuples. We define the following DB functions for actions in QEPs:

```
(scan R)          =   (if (empty? R) *empty*
                          (out (first R) (scan (rest R)))))


(search pred? I)  =   (access_index pred? I)


(filter stream)   =   (if (empty? stream) *empty*
                          (if (pred? (first stream))
                              (out (first stream)
                                   (filter (rest stream)))
                              (filter (rest stream))))


(get stream)      =   (if (empty? stream) *empty*
                          (out (get_tuple REL (first stream))
                               (get (rest stream))))


(project stream)  =   (if (empty? stream) *empty*
                          (out (prj (first stream))
                               (project (rest stream))))
```

```
(ljoin str1 str2) =  (if (empty? str1) *empty*
                         (union (jn (first str1) str2)
                                (ljoin (rest str1) str2)))


(jn ele stream)  =  (if (empty? stream)  *empty*
                       (if (join? ele (first stream))
                          (out (conc ele (first stream))
                               (jn ele (rest stream)))
                          (jn element (rest stream)))))


(union str1 str2) = (if (empty? str1) str2
                       (out (first str1)
                            (union (rest str1) str2)))
```

Note that all functions, except search, return streams of tuples as their result.
Function search provides access to a table containing only those tuples which
satisfy the predicate pred?. Its definition indicates this difference; it is not
defined in terms of stream functions; instead search is mapped directly into the
function access_index provided by the PDBP.

The definitions of functions scan, project, filter, get, jn, and union
all have a common form which is called *linear recursive form*. The definition for
function f has a *linear recursive form* if f is the only recursive function symbol
in its body. For example, function ljoin accesses two streams and its definition
reflects the functional decomposition. Function jn joins the first tuple of the first
stream with all tuples of the second. The union function concatenates the result
of jn with the set of tuples resulting from the recursive call to ljoin. The form
of ljoin's definition is called *extended linear recursive*. A function (f t1) has
an *extended linear recursive form*[1] if its definition

- has a linear recursive form, or

---

[1] Our definition of extended linear recursive form is more general than the definition in [Coh80].

21

- it has the form (f1 t1 (f (f2 t1))) where f1 denotes a function whose definition has an extended linear recursive form, and f2 is a nonrecursive function, or

- it is the composition of two extended linear recursive functions f1 and f2 that are independent of each other, i.e. f1 does not call f2 in its definition and *vice versa*.

For example, functions f1 and f2 are defined for ljoin as follows:

```
(f1 t1 t2) = (if (empty? t1) *empty*
                 (union (jn (first t1)) t2))


(f2 t1)    = (rest t1)
```

f1 still has an extended linear recursive form since its definition is the composition of the two linear recursive functions union and jn. We shall discuss the form of functions further in Section 3.3.2.

The reader may have noticed the difference in the number of arguments for actions *FILTER, PROJECT, GET* and *LJOIN*, and their implementing functions filter, project, get, and ljoin respectively. The first parameter of these actions does not occur as a parameter in the corresponding function. *Not including the parameters in the definition header will simplify the later transformation significantly.* Instead, these parameters are "compiled into" the DB functions. We denote the specialized functions by filter1, project1, get1, and ljoin1. For example, consider the action *(FILTER PRED$_1$? set)*. The corresponding DB function (filter1 stream) is defined as

```
(if (empty? stream) *empty*
    (if (pred1? (first stream))
        (out (first stream) (filter1 (rest stream)))
        (filter1 (rest stream)))))
```

Function filter1 calls pred1? in its definition. filter1 may be viewed as a "specialized" version of the function filter since the function pred1?, implementing predicate *PRED$_1$?*, replaces the general function pred?. Similarly, functions **project** and **get** have compiled into their definition the function prj and the relation REL, respectively. The specialization of function ljoin calls function jn1 which calls function join1? as the implementation of the join predicate $JOIN_1$?.

Example 3

The QEP of example 2 on page 12 translates into the DB expression

```
(project1 (ljoin1 (get1 (scan (search pred0? ISTAT)))
                  (filter1 (scan PAPERS)))))
```

with

```
(project1 str) = (if (empty? str) *empty*
                     (out (prj1 (first str))
                          (project1 (rest str))))

(get1 str)     = (if (empty? str) *empty*
                     (out (get_tuple EMP (first str))
                          (get1 (rest str))))

(filter1  str) = (if (empty? str) *empty*
                     (if (pred1? (first str))
                         (out (first str) (filter1 (rest str)))
                         (filter1 (rest str))))

(ljoin1 str1 str2) = (if (empty? str1) *empty*
                         (union (jn1 (first str1) str2)
                                (ljoin1 (rest str1) str2)))

(jn1 ele str)  = (if (empty? str) *empty*
                     (if (join1? ele (first str))
                         (out (conc ele (first str))
                              (jn1 ele (rest str)))
                         (jn1 ele (rest str))))
```

23

where

pred0?	implements the predicate	(Status = $PROF$)
pred1?	implements the predicate	(Year > 1980)
join1?	implements the predicate	(Emp# = Emp#)
prj1	implements the projection list	(Name)

□

For later reference we define the following sets and mappings between them. Let $\mathcal{F}_{DB}$ denote the set of all DB functions, i.e.

$$\mathcal{F}_{DB} = \{scan,\ search,\ get,\ filter,\ project,\ ljoin,\ jn,\ union\}$$

The mapping from actions for QEPs to their corresponding DB functions is denoted by $\phi : O_{QEP} \longrightarrow \mathcal{F}_{DB}$. If $F \in O_{QEP}$ then $\phi(F) = f$ where $f \in \mathcal{F}_{DB}$. For actions $FILTER$, $PROJECT$, GET, and $LJOIN$ the above explanations apply. Let L_{QEP} denote the set of all QEPs and L_{DB} denote the set of all DB expressions. The mapping between QEPs and DB expressions, which implicitly uses ϕ, is defined by $\Phi : L_{QEP} \longrightarrow L_{DB}$. We shall use this notation later in the definition of the transformation algorithm.

3.2 Simplification Rules and their Properties

This section introduces a term rewriting system which simplifies expressions in the language defined in Section 2.3. The rewriting system will form the *simplification step* of the transformation algorithm presented in Subsection 3.3.5. The rules of this term rewriting system generate a canonical form for each expression with a minimal number of conditional expressions and only one output stream. The rules lead to actual parameters for function expressions which are either constants, variables or function expressions. More formally, let $\mathcal{F}_P$ be the set of all function symbols with

$$\mathcal{F}_P = O_{PDBP} \cup \{if,\ true,\ false,\ conc\} \cup \mathcal{PAR}$$

where $\mathcal{PAR}$ represents the set of all possible functions derived from parameters of the actions in QEPs. Let $\mathcal{V}_P$ denote the set of all variables and $\mathcal{T}_P$ the set

24

of all expressions over $\mathcal{F}_P$ and $\mathcal{V}_P$. Then we define the term rewriting system $(\mathcal{T}_P, \mathcal{R}_P)$ where $\mathcal{R}_P$ contains the following rules:

Rule I: function exchange rule

$$((z\ (if\ t_1\ t_2\ t_3)) \longrightarrow (if\ t_1\ (z\ t_2)\ (z\ t_3)))$$

Rules IIa and IIb: deletion rules

$$((if\ t_1(\ldots(if\ t_1\ t_2\ t_3)\ldots)\ t_4) \longrightarrow (if\ t_1(\ldots\ t_2\ \ldots)\ t_4))$$

$$((if\ t_1\ t_2\ (\ldots(if\ t_1\ t_3\ t_4)\ldots)) \longrightarrow (if\ t_1\ t_2\ (\ldots\ t_4\ \ldots)))$$

Rule III: distribution rule

$$((if\ (if\ t_1\ t_2\ t_3)\ t_4\ t_5) \longrightarrow (if\ t_1\ (if\ t_2\ t_4\ t_5)\ (if\ t_3\ t_4\ t_5)))$$

Rules IVa and IVb: true/false rules

$$((if\ true\ t_1\ t_2) \longrightarrow t_1)$$

$$((if\ false\ t_1\ t_2) \longrightarrow t_2)$$

Rules Va, Vb, Vc, and Vd: stream rules

$$((first\ (out\ t_1\ t_2)) \longrightarrow t_1)$$

$$((rest\ (out\ t_1\ t_2)) \longrightarrow t_2)$$

$$((empty?\ *\ empty*) \longrightarrow true)$$

$$((empty?\ (out\ t_1\ t_2)) \longrightarrow false)$$

The *function exchange rule* performs the "unwinding" of functions with *one parameter*: these functions are distributed over the conditional expression. Note that we only define the function exchange rule for *one parameter functions*. We shall later show that this rule is sufficient for the transformation of expressions generated from actions. The *deletion rules* apply to conditional expressions; they replace superfluous conditional expressions by either the consequent or the alternate of the eliminated expression. The *distribution rule* simplifies two nested condition expressions. The first pair of stream rules implement partial evaluation for conditional expressions. The remaining rules reflect some semantic knowledge about the stream operators. They help to reduce the number of intermediate results by performing *partial evaluation* on streams. For correctness, we assume

25

the evaluation of any function occurs without side effects. Furthermore, the arguments to all functions are strict [FW76]; any computation to obtain values for function parameters is guaranteed to terminate.

The set of rules in the term rewriting system $(\mathcal{T}_P, \mathcal{R}_P)$ is certainly not the most general one. Other researchers suggest larger sets of rules which can transform more general programs [GK84] [Bel84] [Bir84]. However our set of rules is sufficient to transform all functions and programs derived from QEPs.

Using the theory of term rewriting systems we prove the Church-Rosser property for $(\mathcal{T}_P, \mathcal{R}_P)$. According to theorem 2.1 in Section 2.3 it suffices to show that $(\mathcal{T}_P, \mathcal{R}_P)$ is noetherian and confluent. To prove the noetherian condition we will use the method suggested by Manna and Ness [MN70]. Their method requires the construction of a mapping ψ from the set of expressions onto some well founded set $(\mathcal{S}, >)$. A set $\mathcal{S}$ with a strict partial order $>$ is *well founded* if $\mathcal{S}$ does not contain any infinite sequence $s_1 > s_2 > \ldots$, $s_i \in \mathcal{S}$. For $(\mathcal{T}_P, \mathcal{R}_P)$ to be noetherian all rules $(a \longrightarrow b)$ must satisfy $\psi(a) > \psi(b)$ for any values assigned to variables $t_i \in \mathcal{V}(a)$ (and therefore $\mathcal{V}(b)$). Assume there exists a mapping ψ from expressions of $\mathcal{T}_P$ into $\mathcal{S}$. Suppose $\mathcal{D}$ is an infinite derivation. Then $\mathcal{D}$ can be mapped by ψ into an infinite, strictly descending sequence in $\mathcal{S}$, which contradicts the well foundedness of $\mathcal{S}$. If ψ exists, the well founded set $\mathcal{S}$ implies the finiteness of every derivation sequence $\mathcal{D}$. For our purpose we define the mapping ψ_P from expressions in $\mathcal{T}_P$ into the natural numbers $\mathcal{N}$ as follows:

- if f is a constant then $\psi_P(f) = 2$

- if f is an unary function then $\psi_P((f\ t_1)) = 2 * \psi_P(t_1)$

- if f is an binary function then $\psi_P((f\ t_1\ t_2)) = \psi_P(t_1) + \psi_P(t_2)$

- if f is the *if* function then $\psi_P((if\ t_1\ t_2\ t_3)) = \psi_P(t_1) * (\psi_P(t_2) + \psi_P(t_3) + 1)$

The mapping ψ_P assigns the following values to the left and right hand side of any rule in $\mathcal{R}_P$:

I: $((z\ (if\ t_1\ t_2\ t_3)) \longrightarrow (if\ t_1\ (z\ t_2)\ (z\ t_3)))$:
$2 * \psi_P(t_1) * (\psi_P(t_2) + \psi_P(t_3) + 1) > \psi_P(t_1) * (2 * \psi_P(t_2) + 2 * \psi_P(t_3) + 1)$

IIa : $((if\ t_1(\ldots(if\ t_1\ t_2\ t_3)\ldots)\ t_4) \longrightarrow (if\ t_1(\ldots t_2 \ldots)\ t_4))$:

$$\psi_P(t_1) * ((\ldots(\psi_P(t_1) * (\psi_P(t_2) + \psi_P(t_3) + 1))\ldots) + \psi_P(t_4) + 1) >$$
$$\psi_P(t_1) * ((\ldots\psi_P(t_2)\ldots) + \psi_P(t_4) + 1)$$

IIb : $((if\ t_1\ t_2\ (\ldots(if\ t_1\ t_3\ t_4)\ldots)) \longrightarrow (if\ t_1\ t_2\ (\ldots t_4 \ldots)))$:

$$\psi_P(t_1) * (\psi_P(t_2) + (\ldots(\psi_P(t_1) * (\psi_P(t_3) + \psi_P(t_4) + 1))\ldots) + 1) >$$
$$\psi_P(t_1) * (\psi_P(t_2) + (\ldots\psi_P(t_4)\ldots) + 1)$$

III : $((if\ (if\ t_1\ t_2\ t_3)\ t_4\ t_5) \longrightarrow (if\ t_1\ (if\ t_2\ t_4\ t_5)\ (if\ t_3\ t_4\ t_5)))$:

$$\psi_P(t_1) * (\psi_P(t_2) + \psi_P(t_3) + 1) * (\psi_P(t_4) + \psi_P(t_5) + 1) >$$
$$\psi_P(t_1) * (\psi_P(t_2) * (\psi_P(t_4) + \psi_P(t_5) + 1) + \psi_P(t_3) * (\psi_P(t_4) +$$
$$\psi_P(t_5) + 1) + 1)$$

IVa : $((if\ true\ t_1\ t_2) \longrightarrow t_1)$:

$$2 * (\psi_P(t_1) + \psi_P(t_2) + 1) > \psi_P(t_1)$$

IVb : $((if\ false\ t_1\ t_2) \longrightarrow t_2)$:

$$2 * (\psi_P(t_1) + \psi_P(t_2) + 1) > \psi_P(t_2)$$

Va $((first\ (out\ t_1\ t_2)) \longrightarrow t_1)$:

$$2 * (\psi_P(t_1) + \psi_P(t_2)) > \psi_P(t_1)$$

Vb : $((rest\ (out\ t_1\ t_2)) \longrightarrow t_2)$:

$$2 * (\psi_P(t_1) + \psi_P(t_2)) > \psi_P(t_2)$$

Vc : $((empty?\ *empty*) \longrightarrow true)$:

$$4 > 2$$

Vd : $((empty?\ (out\ t_1\ t_2)) \longrightarrow false)$:

$$2 * (\psi_P(t_1) + \psi_P(t_2)) > 2$$

By inspection we verify that $\psi_P(a) > \psi_P(b)$ holds for every rule $(a \longrightarrow b) \in \mathcal{R}_P$ for $\psi_P(a), \psi_P(b) > 1$. Therefore

Lemma 3.1 $(\mathcal{T}_P, \mathcal{R}_P)$ *is noetherian.*

We use this lemma to establish the confluence of $(\mathcal{T}_P, \mathcal{R}_P)$. Since $\mathcal{R}_P$ is finite, the set of critical pairs is finite. The following table summarizes all critical pairs for $\mathcal{R}_P$; rules in the row are superimposed on rules in the column:

	I	IIa	IIb	III	IV	V
I	–	1	1	1	1	–
IIa	–	1	2	2	2	–
IIb	–	2	1	2	2	–
III	–	2	2	1	1	–
IV	–	1	1	–	–	–
V	–	–	–	–	–	–

$\mathcal{R}_P$ induces 34 critical pairs (note that row and column for rule IV have to be counted twice) and we compute a selected number of them:

1. Rule IIa superimposed on rule I yields the critical pair (t, t') with

$$t = (z \, (if \, t_1 \, (\ldots t_2 \ldots) \, t_4)) \,, \, t' = (if \, t_1 \, (z \, (\ldots t_2 \ldots)) \, (z \, t_4))$$

The normal form is t'.

2. Rule III superimposed on rule I yields the critical pair (t, t') with

$$t = (z \, (if \, t_1 \, (if \, t_2 \, t_4 \, t_5) \, (if \, t_3 \, t_4 \, t_5)))$$
$$t' = (if \, (if \, t_1 \, t_2 \, t_3) \, (z \, t_4) \, (z \, t_5))$$

The normal form is $(if \, t_1 \, (if \, t_2 \, (z \, t_4) \, (z \, t_5)) \, (if \, t_3 \, (z \, t_4) \, (z \, t_5)))$.

3. Rule IV superimposed on rule I yields the critical pair (t, t') with

$$t = (if \, true \, (z \, t_1) \, (z \, t_2)) \,, \, t' = (z \, a)$$

The normal form is t'.

All other critical pairs also lead to common normal forms; thus, we conclude from the lemma 3.1 and theorem 2.1 that

Theorem 3.1 $(\mathcal{T}_P, \mathcal{R}_P)$ *is confluent.*

The theorem ensures that the final transformation result is independent of the order the rules are applied; it allows us to choose any order of application. We are left with an optimization problem of determining the shortest derivation as the most efficient one for any expression. For example, any transformation of subexpression t_2 in expression $t = (if\ true\ t_1\ t_2)$ is superfluous since the rule IVa eventually reduces t to t_1. More generally, given a term rewriting system $(\mathcal{T},\ \mathcal{R})$ and an expression $t \in \mathcal{T}$, the problem of determining the shortest sequence of rule applications to derive the minimal form is an interesting research problem.

3.3   The Transformation of DB Functions

In the previous two sections we first introduced a set of DB functions implementing actions in QEPs, and described the term rewriting system $(\mathcal{T}_P, \mathcal{R}_P)$ which simplifies expressions of the defined language $\mathcal{T}_P$. In this section we will derive necessary results for the correctness of the transformation algorithm $\mathcal{ID}$, which is presented in Subsection 3.3.5. The three major transformation steps called *substitution*, *simplification*, and *folding* will be introduced in the Subsection 3.3.1. They transform expressions into *ideal forms* which are defined in Subsection 3.3.2. The ideal form allows us to replace recursion by iteration, which we will discuss in Section 3.4. Subsections 3.3.3 and 3.3.4 show that any combination of DB functions and their transformation yields the ideal form.

3.3.1   The Transformation Steps

The transformation of DB expressions proceeds in three major steps. In the first step, each DB function is replaced by the body of its definition using the actual parameters. Let $(f_1\ x_1 \ldots x_{n_1}) = B(f_1)$ and $(f_2\ y_1 \ldots y_{n_2}) = B(f_2)$ be two function definitions with $\mathcal{V}(B(f_1)) \cap \mathcal{V}(B(f_2)) = \emptyset$. Then we define for $i \leq n_1$

$$s(f_1,\ f_2,\ i) = (f_1\ x_1 \ldots x_{i-1}\ (f_2\ y_1 \ldots y_{n_2})\ x_{i+1} \ldots x_{n_1})\ \text{and}$$
$$S(f_1,\ f_2,\ i) = B(f_1)[x_i\ /\ B(f_2)]$$

We call $S(f_1,\ f_2,\ i)$ the *substitution of parameter i*, $i < n_1$, by function f_2 in f_1. $s(f_1,\ f_2,\ i)$ denotes the DB expression where the function expression calling f_2 is substituted for the ith parameter in the function expression calling f_1. For example, let $f_1 = \texttt{project}$ and $f_2 = \texttt{filter1}$, then

$$s(f_1,\ f_2,\ i) = (\texttt{project}\ (\texttt{filter1}\ \texttt{str}))$$

$S(f_1, f_2, i) =$

```
(if (empty? (if (empty? str) *empty*
                  (if (pred1? (first str))
                       (out (first str) (filter1 (rest str)))
                       (filter1 (rest str)))))
     *empty*
     (out (prj (first (if (empty? str) *empty*
                          (if (pred1? (first str))
                               (out (first str)
                                    (filter1 (rest str)))
                               (filter1 (rest str))))))
          (project (rest (if (empty? str) *empty*
                             (if (pred1? (first str))
                                  (out (first str)
                                       (filter1 (rest str)))
                                  (filter1 (rest str))))))))
```

The result of the substitution step allows us to investigate the "interaction" of both functions. When combined, the same function calls with the same parameter may appear more than once. Looking at the example we recognize that functions empty?, first, rest, and pred1? are called several times. The second step, called the *simplification step*, simplifies the above expression. The step uses the term rewriting system (T_P, R_P) introduced in Section 3.2. The rules in R_P rearrange the order of functions without changing the computational behavior of expressions, and eliminate superfluous functions calls. They are applied exhaustively to an expression t deriving its *minimal form*. We denote the minimal form under (T_P, R_P) by $SIM(t)$. The minimal form for the expression in the above example is

```
(if (empty? str) *empty*
    (if (pred1? (first str))
         (out (prj (first str))
              (project (filter1 (rest str))))))
```

```
(if (empty? (filter1 (rest str))) *empty*
    (out (prj (first (filter1 (rest str))))
         (project (rest (filter1 (rest str)))))))))))
```

This expression already contains fewer operations than the original one. However its form shows the need for a *third* transformation step. We would like to derive an expression which refers only to str, (first str), and (rest str). The function expressions (first (filter1 (rest str))) and (rest (filter1 (rest str))) should be eliminated. We recognize that the subexpression

```
(if (empty? (filter1 (rest str))) *empty*
    (out (prj (first (filter1 (rest str))))
         (project (rest (filter1 (rest str))))))))
```

resembles the body of the function definition for the function project using the actual parameter (filter1 (rest str)). The third step, called *folding*, replaces the subexpression by the function expression (project (filter1 (rest str))) yielding the final expression

```
(if (empty? str) *empty*
    (if (pred1? (first str))
        (out (prj (first str))
             (project (filter1 (rest str))))
        (project (filter1 (rest str)))))
```

Formally, let $t \in \mathcal{T}_P$ and let $\mathcal{G}$ be a set of defined functions. For any two functions $f_i, f_j \in \mathcal{G}$, $i \neq j$, f_i's function body is different from f_j's function body, i.e. $B(f_i) \not\sim B(f_j)$, and f_i's function body cannot be derived from f_j's function body using $(\mathcal{T}_P, \mathcal{R}_P)$. Assume that there exists a subexpression t'' in t such that $t'' = B(f)[x_1/t_1 \ldots x_n/t_n]$ for some function $f \in \mathcal{G}$ where $x_1 \ldots x_n$ are the variables in f. If we replace t'' by the function expression $(f\ t_1 \ldots t_n)$ we derive a new expression t'. We say that $\mathcal{G}$ folds t by f deriving t'. If f exists the restrictions on functions in $\mathcal{G}$ ensure that the result of the folding step is unique. We use the notation $\mathcal{FL}(t, \mathcal{G})$ to denote the expression t' which results from exhaustively folding t by functions in $\mathcal{G}$.

31

3.3.2 Forms of Expressions

This subsection describes the *form* of expressions which are derived by the three transformation steps. We introduce *1-recursive functions* and *ideal forms*. Intuitively, a function f of arity n is called 1-recursive if the recursion occurs only on *one* parameter. The parameter is called the *recursive parameter*; all other parameters are called *constant* parameters. Constant parameters may be needed by functions called in the body of f. For example, the definition of ljoin uses two parameters: str1 is the recursive parameter; str2 is the constant parameter needed to call function jn.

Definition 3.1 *Let* $(f\ x_1 \dots x_n) = B(f)$ *be a linear recursive function* f. *If there exists a function* f1 *with* $n+1$ *parameters such that* $f \notin F(B(\text{f1}))$, $\text{f1} \notin F(B(f))$, *and* $B(f) = B(\text{f1})[x_{n+1} / (f\ x_1 \dots x_{i-1}\ (\text{f2}\ x_i)\ x_{i+1} \dots x_n)]$ *for some* f2 *then* f *is called 1-recursive in parameter* i, $i \leq n$.[2]

For example, function ljoin is 1-recursive in its first parameter. Function f2 is equal to rest and function f1 is defined by

```
(f1 t1 t2 t3) = (if (empty? t1) *empty*
                    (union (jn (first t1) t2) t3))
```

Proposition 3.1 *All DB functions are 1-recursive.*

For the composition of functions we introduce the notion of *ideal form*. The ideal form precisely describes the form of expression we would like to derive from DB expressions by all three transformation steps. The form guarantees the replacement of recursion by iteration. We shall prove in Subsections 3.3.3 and 3.3.4 that the three steps achieve this transformation goal. The ideal form also enables us to define a *new 1-recursive function* which computes the same result as the combination of two 1-recursive functions. For example, consider the expression (project (filter1 str)) used in the previous subsection to derive the expression

---

[2][Coh80] calls these functions "non-ordered, totally ordered".

```
(if (empty? str) *empty*
    (if (pred1? (first str))
        (out (prj (first str))
             (project (filter1 (rest str))))
        (project (filter1 (rest str)))))
```

We introduce the new function

$$(\text{project\_filter1 str}) = (\text{project (filter1 str)})$$

and derive its definition by replacing all occurrences of (project (filter1 str)) by (project_filter1 str) in the above expression, thus yielding the 1-recursive function

```
(project_filter str) =
    (if (empty? str) *empty*
        (if (pred1? (first str))
            (out (prj (first str))
                 (project_filter1 (rest str)))
            (project_filter1 (rest str))))
```

In the following sections we shall often use the combination of functions and the derived expression as a new function as described in the example above. The following definition introduces the ideal form for the combination of functions.

Definition 3.2 *Let* $(f_1\, x_1 \ldots x_{n_1}) = B(f_1)$, $(f_2\, y_1 \ldots y_{n_2}) = B(f_2)$ *be 1-recursive in parameters* i, j, *respectively, with* $f_2 \notin F(B(f_1))$, $f_1 \notin F(B(f_2))$ *and* $t' = s(f_1,\, f_2,\, i)$. *If there exists a function* **f'** *with* $n_1 + n_2$ *parameters such that* $t'' = B(\mathbf{f'})\, [x_{n_1+n_2}\, /\, (f_1\, x_1 \ldots x_{i-1}\, (f_2\, y_1 \ldots (\mathbf{f''}\, y_j) \ldots y_{n_2})\, x_{i+1} \ldots x_{n_1})]$ *for some* **f''** *that computes the same result as* t', *then we say* $s(f_1,\, f_2,\, i)$ *has an ideal form* t''.

Let $\mathcal{I}$ denote the set of all $s(f_i,\, f_j,\, k)$ for which an ideal form exists. If $s(f_i,\, f_j,\, k) \in \mathcal{I}$ then we may define a new 1-recursive function

33

$(\mathbf{g}\ x_1 \ldots x_{i-1}\ x_{i+1} \ldots x_{n_1}\ y_1 \ldots y_{n_2})$ with

$$B(\mathbf{g}) = B(\mathbf{f'})\ [x_{n_1+n_2}\ /\ (\mathbf{g}\ x_1 \ldots x_{i-1}\ x_{i+1} \ldots x_{n_1}\ y_1 \ldots (\mathbf{f''}\ y_j) \ldots y_{n_2})].$$

We say that $s(f_i,\ f_j,\ k)$ *yields* a 1-recursive function. For the above example $\mathbf{f''}$ = rest and

```
(f' t1 t2) = (if (empty? str) *empty*
                 (if (pred1? (first t1))
                     (out (prj (first t1)) t2) t2))
```

Using the transformation as an *operation* on functions we shall prove in the next two subsections that the set of 1-recursive functions is *closed* under the operation transformation. For the proofs we distinguish three different kinds of DB functions according to the structure of their body:

```
(f1 e1 ... em str1) =
    (if (empty? str1) *empty*
        (out (g1 e1 ... em (first str1))
            (f1 e1 ... em (rest str1))))


(f2 e1 ... em str2) =
    (if (empty? str2) *empty*
        (if (pred? (first str2))
            (out (g2 e1 ... em (first str2))
                (f2 e1 ... em (rest str2)))
            (f2 e1 ... em (rest str2))))


(f3 e1 ... em str3 str4) =
    (if (empty? str3) *empty*
        (union (g3 e1 ... em (first str3) str4)
            (f3 e1 ... em (rest str3) str4)))
```

The set of functions of the above form are denoted by $\mathcal{F}_I$, $\mathcal{F}_{II}$, and $\mathcal{F}_{III}$. e1 ... em denote m constant parameters representing elements where m may be zero. All DB functions are either of the form *I*, *II*, or *III*. DB functions in $\mathcal{F}_I$ or $\mathcal{F}_{II}$ are called *1-stream functions*, their general form is

34

```
(f e1 ... em str) =
    (if (empty? str) *empty*
        (if (pred1? (first str))
            (if (pred2? (first str))

                ...

                    (out (g1 e1 ... em (first str))
                        (f e1 ... em (rest str)))
                    (f e1 ... em (rest str))

                ...

                (f e1 ... em (rest str)))
            (f e1 ... em (rest str)))))
```

f may have m constant parameters, and k predicates, $m \geq 0$, $k \geq 0$. Similarly, all DB functions in $\mathcal{F}_{III}$ are called *2-stream functions*. In general for $n \geq 2$, *n-stream function* f is of the form[3]

```
(f e1 ... em str1 ... strn) =
    (if (empty? str1) *empty*
        (if (pred1? (first str))
            (if (pred2? (first str))

                ...

                    (union (g e1 ... em (first str1)
                                        str2 ... strn))
                        (f e1 ... em (rest str1)
                                        str2 ... strn)))
                    (f e1 ... em (rest str))

                ...

                (f e1 ... em (rest str)))
            (f e1 ... em (rest str)))))
```

where g1 represents some tuple function with $f \notin F(B(g1))$. Note that n-stream functions are 1-recursive and have an ideal form.

---

[3]Without loss of generality we assume that recursion occurs on the first stream.

3.3.3 The Transformation of 1-stream Functions

The lemmas and corollaries in this subsection show that any combination of
1-stream functions has an ideal form and yields a 1-stream function.

Lemma 3.2 : *If f_1, $f_1' \in \mathcal{F}_I$, then their combination $s(f_1, f_1', 1)$ has an ideal
form derivable by $\mathcal{UF}$ and $\mathcal{SIM}$.*

Proof :

> As $(\mathcal{T}_P, \mathcal{R}_P)$ is CR it is sufficient to find one rule sequence $\mathcal{D}_R$ which leads
> to a ideal form for $s(f_1, f_1', 1)$.
> Let $\mathcal{D}_R = (I,\ III,\ Vc,\ Vd,\ IVa,\ IVb,\ IIb,\ IIb,\ Va,\ Vb)$ yielding

```
(if (empty? str1) *empty*
    (out (g1 (g1' (first str1)))
         (f1 (f1'(rest str1))))))
```

which is an ideal form with

```
(f' t1 t2) = (if (empty? t1) *empty*
                 (out (g1 (g1' (first t1))) t2))
```

Folding leaves the ideal form unchanged. □

Corollary 3.1 *The combination of two 1-stream functions f_1, $f_1' \in \mathcal{F}_I$ yields a
1-stream function.*

Lemma 3.3 *If $f_1, \in \mathcal{F}_I$, $f_2 \in \mathcal{F}_{II}$, then any of their combinations have an ideal
form derivable by $\mathcal{UF}$, $\mathcal{SIM}$ and $\mathcal{FL}$.*

Proof :

> Consider the case of $s(f_1, f_2, 1)$:
> Using the simplification $\mathcal{SIM}$ the rule sequence
> $\mathcal{D}_R = (\ I,\ I,\ III,\ III,\ Vc,\ Vd,\ IVa,\ IVb,$
> $\qquad\qquad IIb,\ IIb,\ IIb,\ IIa,\ IIa,\ IIb,\ Va,\ Vb)$ yields

```
(if (empty? str2) *empty*
    (if (pred? (first str2))
        (out (g1 (g2 (first str2)))
             (f1 (f2 (rest str2))))
        (if (empty? (f2 (rest str2)))
            (out (g1 (first (f2 (rest str2))))
                 (f1 (rest (f2 (rest str2)))))))))))
```

The folding of the expression by f_1 leads to the ideal form:

```
(if (empty? str2) *empty*
    (if (pred? (first str2))
        (out (g1 (g2 (first str2)))
             (f1 (f2 (rest str2))))
        (f1 (f2 (rest str2))))))
```

The case of $s(f_2, f_1, 1)$ is similar. □

Corollary 3.2 *The combination of two functions* $f_1, \in \mathcal{F}_I$, $f_2 \in \mathcal{F}_{II}$ *yields a 1-stream function.*

Lemma 3.4 *If* $f_2, f_2' \in \mathcal{F}_{II}$, *then their combination* $s(f_2, f_2', 1)$ *has an ideal form derivable by* $\mathcal{UF}$, $\mathcal{SIM}$, *and* $\mathcal{FL}$.

Proof : similar to the proof of the lemma 3.3. □

Corollary 3.3 *The combination of two functions* $f_2, f_2' \in \mathcal{F}_{II}$ *yields a 1-stream function.*

Lemma 3.5 *The combination of function* $f_1 \in \mathcal{F}_I \cup \mathcal{F}_{II}$ *with a 1-stream function has an ideal form and yields a 1-stream function.*

Proof :
    Similar to the proofs of lemmas 3.2 to 3.4 and corollaries 3.1 to 3.3 □

3.3.4 The Transformation of 2-stream Functions

Unfortunately, it turns out that the substitution, simplification and folding steps are not sufficient to create the ideal forms for 2-stream functions. Since the definition of *ljoin* uses the *union* operator, DB expressions which include *ljoin* require more manipulation after these three transformation steps have been performed. Consider the DB expression

```
(filter1 (join1 str1 str2))
```

Substitution, simplification and folding yield the expression

```
(if (empty? str1) *empty*
    (filter1 (union (jn1 (first str1) str2)
                    (join1 (rest str1) str2)))))
```

which does not represent an ideal form. Function `filter1` has to be moved over the union function to achieve the ideal form

```
(if (empty? str1) *empty*
    (union (filter1 (jn1 (first str1) str2))
           (filter1 (join1 (rest str1) str2)))))
```

We introduce an additional term rewriting system $(\mathcal{T}_P, \mathcal{R}_U)$ which defines a fourth transformation step, called the *union step*. To correctly define the rules in $\mathcal{R}_U$, we need to introduce *restricted rules*. A restricted rule is denoted by

$$(a \xrightarrow{C} b)$$

where C is a condition containing variables used in a. The rule can only be applied if the condition evaluates to *true* when assigning values to variables in a. Consider the restricted rule

$$((f_2 \ (union \ t_1 \ t_2) \ t_3) \xrightarrow{C} (union \ (f_2 \ t_1 \ t_3) \ (f_2 \ t_2 \ t_3)))$$

where $C = (f_2 \neq union)$. If we apply the rule to the expression

```
(join1 (union str1 str2) str3)
```

38

$f_2 = \texttt{join1}$ evaluating C to *true*. Therefore the rule can be applied yielding the expression

$$(\texttt{union (join1 str1 str3) (join1 str2 str3)})$$

For the term rewriting system $(\mathcal{T}_P, \mathcal{R}_U)$ we define the following set of rules:

$$\mathcal{R}_U = \{ \ ((\text{union (union } t_1\ t_2)\ t_3) \longrightarrow (\text{union } t_1\ (\text{union } t_2\ t_3))),$$
$$((f_1\ (\text{union } t_1\ t_2)) \longrightarrow (\text{union } (f_1\ t_1)\ (f_1\ t_2))),$$
$$((f_2\ (\text{union } t_1\ t_2)\ t_3) \xrightarrow{C} (\text{union } (f_2\ t_1\ t_3)\ (f_2\ t_2\ t_3))),$$
$$((f_2\ t_1\ (\text{union } t_2\ t_3)) \xrightarrow{C} (\text{union } (f_2\ t_1\ t_2)\ (f_2\ t_1\ t_3)))\ \}$$

where $t_i \in \mathcal{V}$, $f_i \in \mathcal{V}$ denote functions of arity one and two, respectively. The last two rules are needed for 2-stream functions such as `ljoin`. For their application we have to exclude function union and impose the restriction $C = (f_2 \neq union)$. Notice that the restriction is important for two reasons: first, if $f_2 = $ union the transformation result is semantically incorrect; second, if $\mathcal{R}_U$ is extended to a term rewriting system $(\mathcal{T}_P, \mathcal{R}_U)$, the result is not noetherian. However, if we allow conditions on rules as restrictions for their application, then

Theorem 3.2 : $(\mathcal{T}_P, \mathcal{R}_U)$ *is noetherian and confluent.*

Proof : To show $(\mathcal{T}_P, \mathcal{R}_P)$ to be noetherian we define $\mu : \mathcal{T}_P \longrightarrow \mathcal{N}$ to be

- $\mu(f_0) = 2$ with $f_0 \in \mathcal{F}_0$
- $\mu((\text{union } t_1\ t_2)) = (\mu(t_1) + 1) * \mu(t_2)$
- $\mu((f_1\ t_1)) = 2^{\mu(t_1)}$
- $\mu((f_2\ t_1\ t_2)) = 2^{\mu(t_1)+\mu(t_2)}$

then for all rules $(a \longrightarrow b) \in \mathcal{R}_U$: $\mu(a) > \mu(b)$. The following table summarizes all critical pairs induced by $\mathcal{R}_U$ to prove confluence (rules in rows are superimposed on rules in columns):

	I	II	III	IV
I	1	1	1	1
II	–	–	–	–
III	–	–	–	1
IV	–	–	1	–

39

For each critical pair (t, t') we can show that the normal form of t is the same as the normal form of t'. □

Let $\mathcal{UF}(t)$ denote the expression resulting from applying $(\mathcal{T}_P, \mathcal{R}_P)$ to t. We are now ready to show that the combination and transformation of 1-stream and 2-stream functions yields an ideal form using the substitution, simplification, folding, and the union transformation steps.

Lemma 3.6 *If $f_1 \in \mathcal{F}_I$, $f_3 \in \mathcal{F}_{III}$, then all their combinations have an ideal form derivable by $\mathcal{UF}$, $\mathcal{SIM}$, $\mathcal{FL}$, and $\mathcal{UN}$.*

Proof :

First, consider the case $s(f_1, f_3, 1)$:

After unfolding, the simplification by

$\mathcal{D}_R = (I,\ III,\ Vc,\ IVa,\ IIb,\ IIb)$ yields

```
(if (empty? str3) *empty*
        (if (empty? (union (f3' (first str3) str4)
                           (f3 (rest str3) str4)))
            *empty*
            (out (g1 (first (union (f3' (first str3) str4)
                                   (f3 (rest str3) str4))))
                 (f1 (rest (union (f3' (first str3) str4)
                                  (f3 (rest str3) str4)))))))
```

The expression folds by f_1

```
(if (empty? str3) *empty*
        (f1 (union (f3' (first str3) str4)
                   (f3 (rest str3) str4))))
```

The application of the union step leads to the ideal form

```
(if (empty? str3) *empty*
        (union (f1 (f3' (first str3) str4))
               (f1 (f3 (rest str3) str4))))
```

case $s(f_3,\ f_1,\ 1)$:

Let $\mathcal{D}_R = (I,\ III,\ Vc,\ Vd,\ IVa,\ IVb,\ IIb,\ IIb,\ IIb,\ Va,\ Vb)$ yielding

```
(if (empty? str1) *empty*
    (union (g3 (g1 (first str1)) str4)
           (f3 (f1 (rest str1)) str4)))
```

$\mathcal{FL}$ and $\mathcal{UN}$ leave the expression unchanged.

The case of $s(f_3,\ f_1,\ 2)$ is similar. $\square$

Corollary 3.4 *Any combination of the two functions* $f_1 \in \mathcal{F}_I$, $f_3 \in \mathcal{F}_{III}$ *yields a 2-stream function.*

Lemma 3.7 *If* $f_2 \in \mathcal{F}_{II}$, $f_3 \in \mathcal{F}_{III}$, *then all their combinations have an ideal form derivable by* $\mathcal{UF}$, $\mathcal{SIM}$, $\mathcal{FL}$, *and* $\mathcal{UN}$.

Proof :

Similar to the proof of the lemma 3.6. $\square$

Corollary 3.5 *Any combination of the two functions* $f_2 \in \mathcal{F}_{II}$, $f_3 \in \mathcal{F}_{III}$ *yields a 2-stream function.*

Lemma 3.8 *If* $f_3,\ f_3' \in \mathcal{F}_{III}$, *then all their combinations have an ideal form derivable by* $\mathcal{UF}$, $\mathcal{SIM}$, $\mathcal{FL}$, *and* $\mathcal{UN}$.

Proof :

Consider the case $s(f_3,\ f_3',\ 1) = $ (f3 (f3' str3 str4) str5):

The simplification by $\mathcal{D}_R = (I,\ III,\ Vc,\ IVa,\ IIb,\ IIb)$ yields

```
(if (empty? str3) *empty*
    (if (empty? (union (g3' (first str3) str4)
                       (f3' (rest str3) str4))) *empty*
        (union
          (g3 (first (union (g3' (first str3) str4)
                            (f3' (rest str3) str4))) str5)
          (f3 (rest (union (g3' (first str3) str4)
                           (f3' (rest str3) str4))) str5))))
```

41

Folding f3 leads to the expression

```
(if (empty? str3) *empty*
    (f3 (union (g3' (first str3) str4)
               (f3' (rest str3) str4)) str5))
```

Finally, step $\mathcal{UN}$ yields the ideal form

```
(if (empty? str3) *empty*
    (union (f3 (g3' (first str3) str4) str5)
           (f3 (f3' (rest str3) str4) str5)))
```

Consider the case $s(f_3, f_3', 2) = (f3\ str3\ (f3'\ str4\ str5))$:
None of the rules in $\mathcal{R}_P$ can be applied to $S(f_3, f_3', 2)$. Folding f_3' yields
the expression

```
(if (empty? str3) *empty*
    (union (g3 (first str3)(f3' str4 str5))
           (f3 (rest str3) (f3' str4 str5))))
```

which has the desired ideal form. □

Corollary 3.6 *Any combination of the two functions* f_3, $f_3' \in \mathcal{F}_{III}$ *yields a*
3-stream function.

Lemma 3.9 *The combination of n functions* $f_1 \ldots f_n \in \mathcal{F}_{III}$ *has an ideal form*
and yields an $n + 1$ *stream function.*

Proof :
We perform induction on the number of 2-stream functions.

- If $n = 0$, we use lemma 3.8 and corollary 3.6 to achieve the desired
  form
  for the first case:

  ```
  (h str1 str2 str3) = (f3 (f3' str1 str2) str3)
  (h' ele str2 str3) = (f3 (g3 ele str2) str3)
  ```

  for the second case:

42

```
(h str1 str2 str3) = (f3  str1 (f3' str2 str3))
(h' ele str2 str3) = (f3 ele (g3 str2 str3))
```

- Suppose the lemma holds for $n = i$, then if $n = i + 1$ the proofs for cases

```
(f3 str1 (f tr2 ... stri+2))
(f3 (f str1 ... stri+1) stri+2)
```

are similar to the proof of lemma 3.8. We prove the third case with

```
(f3 (h1 str1 ... strk+1) (h2 str1' ... strj+1'))
```

where h1 (h2) is the combination of k $(i - k)$ 2-stream functions with the above form by induction hypothesis. Unfolding, simplification by rules I, III, Vc, IVa, IIb, folding on f3 and h2 and the union step yield the expression

```
(if (empty? str1) *empty*
    (union (f3 (h1' (first str1) str2 ... strk+1)
               (h2 str1' ... strj+1'))
           (f3 (h1 (rest str1) str2 ... strk+1)
               (h2 str1' ... strj+1')))))
```

Now define

```
(h str1 ... strk+1 str1' ... strj+1) =
    (f3 (h1 str1 ... strk+1) (h2 str1' ... strj+1))
(h' ele str2 ... strk+1 str1' ... strj+1) =
    (f3 (h1' ele str2 ... strk+1)
        (h2 str1' ... strj+1))
```

which yields the form of an $i + 2$ streams. $\square$

Another interesting result follows from this lemma which will be used in the transformation algorithm: an n-stream function is evaluated by calling an $n - 1$-stream function and calling itself recursively.

Lemma 3.10 *The combination of function $f_1 \in \mathcal{F}_I \cup \mathcal{F}_{II}$ with a n-stream function has an ideal form and yields a n-stream function.*

Proof :

Similar to the proofs of lemmas 3.2, 3.5 and 3.9, and corollaries 3.1 and 3.3. □

Lemma 3.11 *The combination of a 2-stream function with an n-stream function has an ideal form and yields an $n + 1$-stream function.*

Proof :

Similar to the proof of lemma 3.9. □

The following theorem describes the main result of Section 3.3. Its proof follows immediately from the above lemmas.

Theorem 3.3 *The combination of any functions of the form I, II, or III has an ideal form and yields an n-stream function for some n.*

3.3.5   The Simplification Algorithm

Using theorem 3.3 we define algorithm $\mathcal{ID}$ which returns the ideal form for any DB expression. The proofs of the previous lemmas indicate how to compute the ideal form: If $t = (f_1 \ (f_2 \ (f_3 \ str)))$, then the ideal form for $(f_2 \ (f_3 \ str)))$ is computed first before the combination with f_1 is encountered.

ALGORITHM $\mathcal{ID}$:

Input: DB expression t **Output:** ideal form

Assume all table names are unique.

if $t = (f_1\ t_1)$ and t is a table name: /* case 1 */

$\qquad return\ (\ B(f_1)[str1\ /\ t_1]);$

if $t = (f_1\ t_1)$ and t is a nested DB expression: /* case 2 */

$\qquad l_1 := \mathcal{ID}(t_1);$
$\qquad return\ (\mathcal{UN}\ (\mathcal{FL}\ (\mathcal{SIM}\ (B(f_1)\ [str1\ /\ l_1]))), \{f_1,\ t_1\}));$

if $t = (f_1\ t_1\ t_2)$:   /* case 3 */

$\qquad l_1 := \mathcal{ID}(t_1);$
$\qquad l_2 := \mathcal{ID}(t_2);$
$\qquad return\ (\mathcal{UN}\ (\mathcal{FL}\ (\mathcal{SIM}\ (B(f_1)[str1\ /\ l_1\ ,\ str2\ /\ l_2]))), \{f_1,\ t_1,\ t_2\}));$

In case (1) of the algorithm, we have reached the bottom of the recursion and do not need any simplification or folding. The algorithm simply returns the body of the function with the actual parameter substituted. Cases (2) and (3) take care of the combination with a 1-stream and a 2-stream function, respectively. In both cases variables t_1 and t_2 represent

3.4   Recursion Removal

The final transformation step which we propose for the improvement of programs replaces recursion by iteration. While the recursive form of programs supports clear programming style and simplifies program manipulation it may not be the most efficient form for program execution [Coh80] [BD77]. Cohen gives a comprehensive overview on various recursive forms and their transformation into iteration[Coh80]. However, these kinds of transformations are not always necessary to guarantee efficient execution. Steele implements certain forms of recursion efficiently by improved stack management [Ste77].

This section discusses the replacement of extended linear recursion by iteration using the transformation schemes suggested by [BD77]. Let f be a linear recursive function of the form

```
(f t1) = (if (pred? t1) f1
              (f2 (f3 t1) (f (f4 t1)))))
```

with $f \notin F(B(f2)) \cup F(B(f3)) \cup F(B(f4))$. If f2 satisfies the condition

```
(f2 t1 (f2 t2 t3)) = (f2 t2 (f2 t1 t3))
```

then f can be transformed into the iterative program

```
((set result f1)
 (DO (t t1 (f4 t))
     (pred? t)
     (set result (f2 (f3 t) result)))))
```

The iterative form introduces the variable result which *accumulates* the intermediate results on each call of f2. The variable is initialized to f1, to the "bottom" value of the recursion.

Lemma 3.12 *The ideal form of any combination of DB functions yields an iterative program using the above recursion scheme.*

Proof : The proof immediately follows from the definitions of a 1-recursive function and the ideal form together with theorem 3.3. Since the order of tuples is irrelevant, functions *out* and *union* satisfy the above condition for f2. □

For example, for any function $f \in \mathcal{F}_I$, f1 = *empty*, f4 = rest, f2 = out, and (f3 t) = (g1 (first t)) which yields the iterative program

```
((set result *empty*)
 (DO (t str1 (rest t))
     (empty? t)
     (set result (out (g1 (first t)) result)))))
```

46

For $f \in \mathcal{F}_{II}$, f1 =*empty*, f3=rest, f4 = rest, and

```
(f2 t1 t2) = (if (pred? (first t1))
                 (out (first t1) t2) t2)
```

yielding the corresponding iterative program

```
((set result *empty*)
 (DO (t str2 (rest t))
     (empty? t)
     (if (pred? (first t))
         (set result (out (first t) result)))))
```

The program already includes two improvements. First, we distributed the assignment statement over the condition; second, we eliminated the superfluous alternative (set result result) in the condition expression.

For f3 $\in \mathcal{F}_{III}$ the above schema for recursion removal is applied twice. First, we replace the recursion for f3 yielding program P_1

```
((set result *empty*)
 (DO (t str3 (rest t))
     (empty? t)
     (set result (union (f3' (first t) str4) result))))
```

We recognize that P_1 still contains an expression involving a recursive function, namely (union (f3' (first t) str4) result). Assuming that f3' is a linear recursive function in str4 its ideal form is

```
(if (empty? str4) result
    (if (pred? (first t) (first str4))
        (out (g3 (first t) (first str4))
             (union (f3' (first t) (rest str4)) result))
        (union (f3' (first t) (rest str4)) result)))
```

which translates into the iterative program P_2

47

```
((set result' result)
 (DO (t' str4 (rest t'))
     (empty? t')
     (if (pred? (first t) (first t'))
         (set result'
              (out (g3 (first t) (first t')) result')))))
```

Now, all recursive functions have been removed in P_2. To remove the recursion in P_1 we eliminate the statement (set result' result) and change result' to result in P_2, before replacing the assingment statement in P_1 by the modified program P_2. These changes yield the final iterative program for f3

```
((set result *empty*)
 (DO (t str3 (rest t))
     (empty? t)
     (DO (t' str4 (rest t'))
         (empty? t')
         (if (pred? (first t) (first str4))
             (set result
                  (out (g3 (first t) (first t')) result))))))
```

For the transformation algorithm we introduce the mapping $\mathcal{RI}$ which replaces recursion by iteration as follows: Let f be an n-stream function which is 1-recursive on its first stream parameter with

```
(f e1 ... em str1 ... strn) =
   (if (empty? str1) *empty*
       (g3 e1 ... em (first str1) str2 ... strn
           (f e1 ... em (rest str1) str2 ... strn)))
```

for some g3. Then we define $\mathcal{RI}(\mathtt{f}, B(\mathtt{f}))$ to be

```
(DO (t stri (rest t))
    (empty? t)
    (g3 e1 ... em (first t) str2 ... strn  result))
```

3.5 The Transformation Algorithm

Using the different transformation steps developed in the previous sections, we are now ready to present the complete transformation algorithm $T\mathcal{R}_R$:

Let $\hat{e}$ denote the empty expression. Let $\mathcal{R}(t)$ be any subexpression $t' = (f_1\ t_1 \ldots t_n)$ in t such that f_1 is a recursive function and t' is not embedded in another function expression calling a recursive function. If t' does not exist in t, let $\mathcal{R}(t) = \hat{e}$. Function $\mathcal{A}(t\,,\,r)$ applies rule r exhaustively to expression t.

ALGORITHM $T\mathcal{R}_R$:

> **Input:** Query evaluation plan qep **Output:** Iterative program
>
> *begin*
>
> $\quad\quad t = \Phi(qep);\quad t_1\ =\ t;$
> $\quad\quad while\ t_1 \neq \hat{e}\ do$
> $\quad\quad\quad\quad t_2\ \ :=\ \ \mathcal{ID}(t_1);\quad\quad /\ast\ compute\ the\ ideal\ form\ \ast/$
> $\quad\quad\quad\quad t_3\ \ :=\ \ \mathcal{RI}(t_1,\ t_2);\quad /\ast\ generate\ iterative\ expression\ \ast/$
> $\quad\quad\quad\quad t\ \ \ :=\ \ t\,[t_1\,/\,t_3];\quad\ \ /\ast\ replace\ recursion\ by\ iteration\,\ast/$
> $\quad\quad\quad\quad t_1\ \ :=\ \ \mathcal{R}(t)\quad\quad\quad /\ast\ more\ recursion\ ?\ \ast/$
> $\quad\quad end\_do;$
> $\quad\quad /\ast\ generate\ assignment\ statements\ \ast/$
> $\quad\quad t\ \ :=\ \ ((set\ result\ \ast\ empty)\ prg)\ U\,prg\,/\,te;$
> $\quad\quad t\ \ :=\ \ \mathcal{A}(t,\ ((out\ a\ b)\ \longrightarrow\ (set\ result\ (out\ a\ b))))$
>
> *end;*

Theorem 3.4 *Given a QEP qep with n tables, algorithm $T\mathcal{R}_R$ produces an iterative expression with n loops.*

Proof :

> We perform induction on the number of tables and use theorem 3.3. The translation of a QEP with n tables by Φ yields a DB expression with n streams. If $n = 1$, then steps $\mathcal{ID}$ and $\mathcal{RI}$ produce an expression with one loop containing no more recursive functions. If $n = i$, then step $\mathcal{ID}$ produces an ideal form yielding an i-stream function. By theorem 3.3 the

ideal form contains the union of an $i-1$-stream function with itself as the only recursive expression. Step $\mathcal{RI}$ replaces the reference to the i-stream function by the variable $result$ thus leaving an $i-1$-stream expression; by the hypothesis this yields an iterative expression with $i-1$ loops. $\square$

Example 4

Transformation algorithm $\mathcal{TR}_R$ translates the DB expression of example 3 on page 23 as follows. The ideal form produced in the first round is of the form

```
(if (empty? (access_index pred0? ISTAT)) *empty*
    (union
        (project1 (jn1 (first (access_index pred0? ISTAT))
                       (filter1 (scan PAPERS))))
        (project1 (ljoin1 (rest (access_index pred0? ISTAT))
                          (filter1 (scan PAPERS))))))))
```

which yields the iterative program

```
(DO (str1 (access_index pred0? ISTAT) (rest str1))
    (empty? str1)
    (union (project1 (jn1 (get_tuple EMP (first str1))
                          (filter1 (scan PAPERS)))) result)
```

The iterative expression still contains a subexpression calling recursive programs, namely

```
(union (project1 (jn1 (get_tuple EMP (first str))
                      (filter1 (scan PAPERS)))) result)
```

In the next round algorithm $\mathcal{TR}_R$ produces the ideal form

```
(if (empty? PAPERS) result
    (if (pred1? (first PAPERS))
        (if (join1? (get_tuple EMP (first str)) (first PAPERS))
            (out (prj1 (conc (get_tuple EMP (first str))
                             (first PAPERS)))
```

```
                (union (project1 (jn1 (get_tuple EMP (first str))
                                      (filter1 (scan (rest PAPERS)))))
                    result))
            (union (project1 (jn1 (get_tuple EMP (first str))
                                  (filter1 (scan (rest PAPERS)))))
                result))
        (union (project1 (jn1 (get_tuple EMP (first str))
                              (filter1 (scan (rest PAPERS)))))
            result)))
```

Replacing recursion by iteration we obtain

```
(DO (str2 PAPERS (rest str2))
    (empty? str2)
    (if (pred1? (first str2))
        (if (join1? (get_tuple EMP (first str1)) (first str2))
        (out (prj1 (conc (get_tuple EMP (first str))) (first str2))
            result)))
```

Substituting the last iterative expression into the first and adding the result statement yields the final iterative program:

```
((set result *empty*)
 (DO (str1 (access_index pred0? ISTAT) (rest str1))
     (empty? str1)
     (DO (str2 PAPERS (rest str2))
         (empty? str2)
         (if (pred1? (first str2))
             (if (join1? (get_tuple EMP (first str1)) (first str2))
                 (set result
                     (out (prj1 (conc (get_tuple EMP (first str))
                                      (first str2))) result)))))))
```

☐

Algorithm $\mathcal{TR}_R$ combines several techniques of functional programming and program transformation to solve the translation problem of relational queries.

Its elegance and clear structure are contrasted by potentially long computations resulting in inefficient progress for the entire transformation. Consider the following DB expression joining $n + 1$ streams:

```
(JOINn str) = (join1 (join2 ... (joinn str strn) ... str2) str1)
```

with functions

```
(joini str' str'') = (if (empty? str') *empty*
                         (union (jni (first str') str'')
                                (joini (rest str') str'')))
```

The application of step $\mathcal{ID}$ yields the ideal form

```
(if (empty? str1) *empty*
    (union (JOINn-1 (jnn (first str) strn)) (JOINn (rest str))))
```

The $i - 1$st level of the recursion in step $\mathcal{ID}$ calls itself to compute the ideal form for (joini+1 ... (joinn str strn) ... stri+1) before unfolding joini and simplifying the resulting expression. For the ideal form on this level joini is used again for folding. Step $\mathcal{UN}$ yields the ideal form

```
(if (empty? str) *empty*
    (union (joini ... (jnn (first str) strn) ... stri)
           (joini ... (joinn (rest str) strn) ... stri)))
```

which is returned as the result of level i. The alternation of folding and unfolding to "push out" the condition (empty? str) and the empty stream *empty* is repeated on each level i of the recursion, $i < n$. The innermost stream determines the outermost loop, so this alternation is repeated for each iteration in $\mathcal{TR}_R$.

A second inefficiency arises if the stream strj is replaced by a nested subexpression tj. The ith level of recursion in $\mathcal{ID}$ computes the ideal form of t_i. However, the proof of lemma 3.9 shows this computation to be superfluous since tj's ideal form is always folded back to tj to yield the ideal form. tj's ideal form is only needed when the ideal form of (jnj (g (first str) ... (first strj+1)) tj) is computed. Algorithm $\mathcal{ID}$ can be easily changed to avoid these unnecessary computations.

Much of the transformation in the simplification step is concerned with the manipulation of stream functions; whenever two functions are combined, the rules eliminate the intermediate stream which is passed from one function to the other. The rule sequences in the proofs for lemmas 3.2 to 3.11 show that the removal of intermediate streams involves a significant number of steps. This observation suggests that we look for a different representation of DB functions to reduce the number of transformation steps.

3.6 More about Transformation

A major achievements of algorithm $\mathcal{TR}_R$ is its elimination of intermediate streams between calling and called function. This optimization is often called *vertical loop fusion* [GP84]. In this section we investigate another form of loop elimination called *horizontal loop fusion*: two programs which access the same stream are combined into one program with one loop. This new programs now computes both results in "parallel" thus accessing the stream only once.

Consider the DB expression (union (filter1 str1) (filter2 str1)).[4] Using algorithm $\mathcal{ID}$ yields the ideal form

```
(if (empty? str1)
    (filter2 str1')
    (if (pred1? (first str1))
        (out (first str1)
            (union (filter1 (rest str1)) (filter2 str1')))
        (union (filter1 (rest str1)) (filter2 str1'))))
```

Since $\mathcal{ID}$ needs unique stream names, str1 in (filter2 str1) is renamed to str1'. Applying the translation scheme for linear recursive programs twice creates an iterative expression with two loops.

Although algorithm $\mathcal{TR}_R$ does not perform horizontal loop fusion, we show in this section how a new definition of the union operator derives an ideal form for the above DB expression to perform horizontal loop fusion. The trans-

---

[4]This expression is not derivable from any QEP.

formation needs user guidance. Consider the following new definition for the operator union:

```
(union str1 str2) =
        (if (empty? str1) str2
            (out (first str1) (union str2 (rest str1)))))
```

Applying steps $\mathcal{UF}$ and $\mathcal{SIM}$ to the initial DB expression we obtain

```
(if (empty? str1)
    *empty*
    (if (pred1? (first str1))
        (if (pred2? (first str1))
            (out (first str1)
                 (union (out (first str1) (filter2 (rest str1)))
                        (filter1 (rest str1))))
            (out (first str1) (union (filter2 (rest str1))
                                     (filter1 (rest str1)))))
        (if (empty? (filter1 (rest str1)))
            (if (pred2? (first str1))
                (out (first str1) (filter2 (rest str1)))
                (filter2 (rest str1)))
            (if (pred2? (first str1))
                (out (first (filter1 (rest str1)))
                     (union (out (first str1)
                                 (filter2 (rest str1)))
                            (rest (filter1 (rest str1)))))
                (out (first (filter1 (rest str1)))
                     (union (filter2 (rest str1))
                            (rest (filter1 (rest str1)))))))))))
```

The subexpression beginning with (if (empty? (filter (rest str1)))
...) is a potential candidate for folding. Consider the following rule

$$r = ((if\ t_1\ (if\ t_2\ t_3\ t_4)(if\ t_2\ t_5\ t_6)) \longrightarrow (if\ t_2\ (if\ t_1\ t_3\ t_5)(if\ t_1\ t_4\ t_6)))$$

Note that if we include r in the rule set $\mathcal{R}_P$ then $(\mathcal{T}_P, \mathcal{R}_P)$ is no longer noetherian since r is its own inverse. Applying r *once* to the above subexpression yields the expression

```
(if (empty? str1)
    *empty*
    (if (pred1? (first str1))
        (if (pred2? (first str1))
            (out (first str1)
                (union (out (first str1) (filter2 (rest str1)))
                    (filter1 (rest str1))))
            (out (first str1)
                (union (filter2 (rest str1))
                    (filter1 (rest str1)))))
        (if (pred2? (first str1))
            (if (empty? (filter1 (rest str1)))
                (out (first str1) (filter2 (rest str1)))
                (out (first (filter1 (rest str1)))
                    (union (out (first str1)
                            (filter2 (rest str1)))
                        (rest (filter1 (rest str1))))))
            (if (empty? (filter1 (rest str1)))
                (filter2 (rest str1))
                (out (first (filter1 (rest str1)))
                    (union (filter2 (rest str1))
                        (rest (filter1 (rest str1)))))))))
```

Now, we can fold **filter1** twice yielding the expression

```
(if (empty? str1)
    *empty*
    (if (pred1? (first str1))
        (if (pred2? (first str1))
            (out (first str1)
                (union (out (first str1) (filter2 (rest str1)))
                    (filter1 (rest str1))))
            (out (first str1)
                (union (filter2 (rest str1))
                    (filter1 (rest str1)))))
```

```
(if (pred2? (first str1))
    (union (filter1 (rest str1))
           (out (first str1) (filter2 (rest str1))))
    (union (filter1 (rest str1)) (filter2 (rest str1))))))))
```

To achieve the ideal form we must perform some additional manipulation. The following three rules best describe the necessary transformation on the previous expression to obtain the ideal form:

$$r_{u_1} = ((\text{union} (\text{out} \ t_1 \ t_2) \ t_3) \longrightarrow (\text{out} \ t_1 \ (\text{union} \ t_2 \ t_3)))$$
$$r_{u_2} = ((\text{union} \ t_1 \ (\text{out} \ t_2 \ t_3)) \longrightarrow (\text{out} \ t_2 \ (\text{union} \ t_1 \ t_3)))$$
$$r_{u_3} = ((\text{union} \ (filter_1 \ t_1) \ (filter_2 \ t_1)) \longrightarrow (\text{union} \ (filter_2 \ t_1) \ (filter_1 \ t_1)))$$

Using $\mathcal{RI}$ the ideal form immediately translates into an iterative expression with one loop:

```
((set result *empty*)
 (DO  (t str1 (rest t))
      (empty? t)
      (if (pred1? (first t))
          (if (pred2? (first t))
              (set result (out (first t) (out (first t) result)))
              (set result (out (first t) result)))
          (if (pred2? (first t))
              (set result (out (first t) result))))))))
```

The transformation result may appear surprising since elements which satisfy both predicates pred1? and pred2? occur twice in the result. However, the loop program reflects the initial specification; the transformation does not include *automatic duplicate elimination*.

Chapter 4

Query Transformation based on Map Expressions

The analysis of algorithm $\mathcal{TR}_R$ in the previous chapter presented our major criticism of the recursion-based transformation approach. The elimination of intermediate streams which occurs when two functions are combined uses too many rules; it accounts for much of the overall transformation effort. Furthermore, the computation of ideal forms may involve long derivations which almost redundantly fold and unfold DB functions.

The two aspects motivated our development of a different formalism which would overcome the described problems without losing the advantages offered by techniques of functional programming and program transformation. The following observation explains one of the reasons for the difficulties encountered: the recursive definition of DB functions intertwines aspects of *control structure information* and *functional* "behavior". Each function definition specifies in a tightly coupled manner *what* has to be computed and *how* to perform the computation. This observation motivated a notation which — at least initially — would clearly separate these two aspects for their manipulation. This chapter first develops such notation together with two transformation systems to manipulate information about the control structure and functional behavior of programs independently. We first translate DB expressions into *map expressions* which emphasize the control structure aspects. Once map expressions have been transformed into a normal form, we translate them into λ-*expressions* to perform *functional combination* which leads to the final iterative program form.

One may conclude from the discussion that the new approach makes the transformation of the previous chapter superfluous. However, the following sections will show that correctness, meaning, and understanding of map expressions are based on the concepts and ideas of the first algorithm. The last section of this chapter compares both approaches and discusses their relationship in more detail.

Map expressions are motivated by the Lisp operator *map*; the operator represents a loop — or linear recursive — control structure without specifying its exact implementation. The meaning of the expression $(map\ f\ list)$ with f being a function of arity one is defined as "applying function f to each element in the list."[1] Similarly, Backus introduced the α-operator in the FP language with the same semantics [Bac78]. Usually, *map* takes a list of elements as its second argument and produces a new list of elements using f. We extend its use to produce *lists of functions* from lists of elements. This aspect is further discussed in the first section.

The *map* operator's high level nature encourages the manipulation of control structure information by a simple, but powerful set of transformation rules. Several researchers have developed different sets of rules to improve the efficiency of FP programs [Bel84] [GK84] [Bir84]. For our purpose we introduce a small set of transformation rules to manipulate map expressions. Its application leads to a final canonical form representing a program with the minimal number of loops necessary to perform the specified evaluation. Map expressions in their canonical form are then translated into iterative expressions of the target language. Another transformation system with rules similar to the ones in $\mathcal{R}_P$ derives the final iterative expressions. We also show that the transformation of map expressions not only achieves vertical loop fusion, but extends to horizontal loop fusion as well. Finally, we briefly describe *query programs* that evaluate more than one query and, if possible, more efficiently by loop fusion.

---

[1] This explanation actually simplifies the description of operator *map*. For example, the second argument could be a list of pairs for a function f of arity two.

4.1 Definition of Functions

This section introduces new definitions of functions for the two level transformation. First, each DB function of the previous chapter is redefined in terms of a map expression for control structure manipulation. Second, we provide another set of functions for functional composition to generate the final iterative expressions.

Before we define DB functions in terms of map expressions we examine in more detail the operator *map* and its use in our context. Instead of lists we use streams for notational uniformity. For convenience we use one element and a stream consisting of only one element interchangeably.

During the transformation different kinds of streams are generated. A *constant stream cstr* is a stream whose elements e_i are constants, i.e. $e_i \in \mathcal{F}_0$. We write $\mathcal{F}_k^n$ to denote the set of streams of length n whose elements are members of $\mathcal{F}_k$. If $k > 0$, we say that $\mathcal{F}_k^n$ is the set of *function streams* of length n whose elements are functions of arity k. A *stream of streams sstr* is defined as a stream of constant streams or a stream of function streams all of which have the same length. If *sstr* contains m streams of length n we write $sstr \in (\mathcal{F}_k^n)^m$. Using an element and a stream of one element interchangeably implies $\mathcal{F}_k^n = (\mathcal{F}_k^1)^n$. Examples of streams are denoted by $str = < e_1, \ldots, e_n >$.

In the introduction of this chapter we described *map* as a function which produces a constant stream by applying a function of arity one to each element of the original constant stream. Our first extension changes the allowable range of functions: Suppose $f_2 \in \mathcal{F}_2$, then the result of $(map\ f_2\ cstr)$ is a *stream of functions fstr*; binding f_2's first argument to each element of *cstr* generates a list of new elements which are functions. The number of functions in *fstr* is equal to the number in *cstr*. For example, let "+" denote the addition operator and $cstr = < 1, 2 >$ then $(map\ +\ cstr)$ produces a stream of two functions of arity one, the first adding 1 to any given argument, the second adding 2. In general we extend *map* to be the function:

$$map\ :\ \mathcal{F}_n \times \mathcal{F}_0^m \longrightarrow \mathcal{F}_{n-1}^m,\ n \geq 1$$

The first extension of *map* naturally leads to a second: instead of providing only one function to *map* we allow its first argument to be a *stream of functions*.

If map applies a stream of functions of arity n to a constant stream the result is a stream of streams whose elements are functions of arity $n-1$. More formally,

$$map : \mathcal{F}_n^k \times \mathcal{F}_0^m \longrightarrow (\mathcal{F}_{n-1}^k)^m, \; n \geq 1$$

To transform streams of streams into streams we introduce the operator $union*$ as a generalization of $union$ to an arbitrary number of arguments. $union*$ applies to streams of constant streams as well as to streams of function streams. Formally, let S^k denote the set of all streams of length k, then

$$union* : (S^k)^m \longrightarrow S^{k*m}$$

that is, $union*$ creates a stream of length $k*m$ from a stream of length m of streams containing k elements. We notice that $union*$ is also defined for streams: Let $str_k^n \in \mathcal{F}_k^n$, then

$$\left(union*\; str_k^n\right) = \left(union*(str_k^1)^n\right) = str_k^n$$

Using the definitions of map and $union*$ we define $map*$ to be

$$(map*\; fstr\; cstr) = (union*\; (map\; fstr\; cstr))$$

The result of $(map*\; fstr\; cstr)$ may be determined by evaluating one element of the function stream $fstr$ against all elements of $cstr$ or vice versa. As the order of elements in streams is irrelevant, both evaluations yield the same result.

A *map expression* $(map*\; f\; cstr)$ is *well formed* if f denotes either a function or a well formed map expression returning a stream of functions and $cstr$ is a constant representing a stream or $cstr$ is a well formed map expression returning a constant stream.

To define DB functions in terms of map expressions we redefine the base functions of Section 2.1: Prj_i denotes the function `prji` which implements the projection of tuples according to parameter PRJ_i for action $PROJECT$. Similarly, $Pred_i?$ denotes function `predi?`, Get_tuple denotes function `get_tuple`. $Cjoin_i?$ represents the combination of functions `joini?` and `conc`. Additionally, we introduce the identity function Id. Using these functions we redefine all DB functions as follows:

$$
\begin{aligned}
(scan\ table) &= (map*\ Id\ table) \\
(search\ pred?\ table) &= (access\_index\ pred?\ table) \\
(get\ table\ stream) &= (map*\ (Get\_tuple\ table)\ stream) \\
(filteri\ str) &= (map*\ Pred_i?\ str) \\
(projecti\ str) &= (map*\ Prj_i\ str) \\
(ljoini\ str1\ str2) &= (map*\ (map*\ (K\ Cjoin_i?)\ str2)\ str1)
\end{aligned}
$$

Note that $Cjoin_i?$ is the only function of arity 2. For the first transformation we assume that the first argument of $Cjoin_i?$ is bound to elements in $str1$; therefore we have to ensure that $(map*\ (K\ Cjoin_i?)\ str2)$ returns a stream with functions whose *second arguments are bound to elements in str2*. Informally, the operator K appearing in the definition of $ljoin$ reverses the arguments of $Cjoin_i?$ to guarantee the correct binding of variables. Later in this section we define operator K more formally.

As we mentioned in the introduction of this chapter, map expressions simplify the manipulation of control structure information. However, the functional composition in the second transformation step cannot be described as elegantly as in the previous chapter. For a formal description we introduce the *lambda notation* (λ-notation) of denotational semantics as presented in [Sto77] and [Ten76]. We restrict its use to the description of functional combination; for more details and further reference see [Sto77], [Ten76], and [Mey82]. The λ-notation becomes necessary to correctly describe functions newly created during the translation from map expressions into λ-expressions. As the number of parameters may vary, all parameters are represented explicitly.

For example, if "+" denotes the addition function then $\lambda t_1.\lambda t_2.(+\ t_1\ t_2)$ is called a *λ-expression*, or *λ-abstraction*, denoting the addition function with its formal parameters. This expression, when applied to the argument 4 yields another function denoted by the λ-expression $\lambda t_2.(+\ 4\ t_2)$ which may be called the "add-four" function. Possible arguments to λ-expression include other λ-expressions to generate new λ-expressions denoting new functions. In general, if $\lambda t_1.u$ is a λ-expression which is *applied* to another λ-expression v the new expression is denoted $u[t_1\ /\ v]$. To avoid naming conflicts we assume the set of variables for both expressions to be disjoint. For our purposes a λ-expression is either any expression of the defined target language or an expression $\lambda t_1.u$ where u is a λ-expression. In the sequel $\mathcal{AP}$ denotes the exhaustive application of λ-expressions.

For functional composition in the second transformation step we define functions Id, Prj_i, Get_tuple, $Pred_i?$, and $Cjoin_i?$ by λ-expressions:

$$
\begin{aligned}
Id &= \lambda t_1.t_1 \\
Prj_i &= \lambda t_1.(prj_i\ t_1) \\
Get\_tuple &= \lambda t_1.t_2.(get\_tuple\ t_1\ t_2) \\
Pred_i? &= \lambda t_1.(if\ (pred_i?\ t_1)\ t_1) \\
Cjoin_i? &= \lambda t_1.t_2.(if\ (join_i?\ t_1\ t_2)\ (conc\ t_1\ t_2))
\end{aligned}
$$

The definitions of $Pred_i?$ and $Cjoin_i?$ do not satisfy our initial intention to provide only *total functions* as arguments to *map**. We could extend both functions to total functions to fulfill the requirement. However, our choice of partial functions will help simplify the transformation significantly.

To formally describe functional composition in map expressions we introduce the operator L which is defined by the λ-expression:

$$(L\ f_1\ f_2) = \lambda t'_1.\ldots.\lambda t'_{n_1}.\lambda t_1.\ldots.\lambda t_{n_1}.\ (f_1\ (f_2\ t'_1\ldots t'_{n_1})\ t_2\ldots t_{n_1})$$

with f_1 and f_2 being functions of arity m and n, respectively. For the application of L's λ-expression to functions f_1 and f_2 we assume that $t_2\ldots t_{n_1}$ and $t'_1\ldots t'_{n_1}$ do not occur as variables in f_1 and f_2. The form of the λ-expression for L can vary depending on the arity of functions f_1 and f_2. The implementation of operator L by its λ-expression ensures that L is associative, i.e. $(L\ f_1\ (L\ f_2\ f_3)) = (L(L\ f_1\ f_2)\ f_3)$. To see this, suppose f_i has arity n_i, $i = 1, 2$, or 3, with $f_i = \lambda t_1.\ldots.t_{n_i}.(g_i\ t_1\ldots t_{n_i})$, then

$$(L\ f_2\ f_3) = \lambda t''_1\ldots.\lambda t''_{n_3}.\lambda t'_2\ldots.\lambda t'_{n_2}.\ (g_2\ (g_3\ t''_1\ldots t''_{n_3})\ t'_2\ldots t'_{n_2})$$

The composition of all three functions under L is

$$
\begin{aligned}
(L\ f_1\ (L\ f_2\ f_3)) =\\
\lambda t''_1.\ldots.\lambda t''_{n_3}.\lambda t'_2.\ldots.\lambda t'_{n_2}.\ \lambda t_2.\ldots.\lambda t_{n_1}.\ (g_1\ (g_2\ (g_3\ t''_1\ldots t''_{n_3})\ t'_2\ldots t'_{n_2})\ t_2\ldots t_{n_1})
\end{aligned}
$$

On the other hand

$$(L \ f_1 \ f_2) \ = \ \lambda t'_1 \ldots \lambda t'_{n_3}.\lambda t_2 \ldots \lambda t_{n_1}. \ (g_1 \ (g_2 \ t'_1 \ldots t'_{n_2}) \ t_2 \ldots t_{n_1})$$

composed with f_3 yields

$$(L \ (L f_1 \ f_2) \ f_3) \ =$$
$$\lambda t''_1 \ldots \lambda t''_{n_3}.\lambda t'_2 \ldots \lambda t'_{n_2}. \ \lambda t_2 \ldots \lambda t_{n_1}. \ (g_1 \ (g_2 \ (g_3 \ t''_1 \ldots t''_{n_3}) \ t'_2 \ldots t'_{n_2}) \ t_2 \ldots t_{n_1})$$

which is identical to $(L \ f_1 \ (L \ f_2 \ f_3))$.

Example :

Consider the expression $(L \ Cjoin_i? \ Prj_i)$. Using the above definitions the expression translates into:

$$\lambda t_1.\lambda t_2. \ ((\lambda t'_1.\lambda t'_2. \ (if \ (join_i? \ t'_1 \ t'_2) \ (conc \ t'_1 \ t'_2))) \ (\lambda \ t''_1. \ (prj_i \ t''_1) \ t_1) \ t_2)$$

Evaluating $(\lambda \ t''_1. \ (prj_i \ t''_1) \ t_1))$ to $(prj_i \ t_1)$ yields the expression

$$\lambda t_1.\lambda t_2. \ ((\lambda t'_1.\lambda t'_2. \ (if \ (join_i? \ t'_1 \ t'_2) \ (conc \ t'_1 \ t'_2))) \ (prj_i \ t_1) \ t_2)$$

Applying $(prj_i \ t_1)$ and t_2 to the inner λ-expression yields the final expression

$$\lambda t_1.\lambda t_2. \ (if \ (join_i? \ (prj_i \ t_1) \ t_2) \ (conc \ (prj_i \ t_1) \ t_2))$$

The expression correctly represents the combination of both functions $Cjoin_i?$ and Prj_i.

The result of operator K was informally described by reversing the argument list for any function f. Using a λ-expression we define the operator by

$$(K \ f_1) \ = \ \lambda t_1.\ldots.t_n. \ (f_1 \ t_n \ldots t_1)$$

for any function f_1 of arity n. Similarly, we introduced *map** as an operator representing a loop-like control structure. We define the operator in terms of a λ-expression for the second transformation step by:

$$(map* \ f_1 \ str) \ =$$

$$\lambda t_2 \ldots t_n. \ (do \ (t_1 \ str \ (rest \ t_1)) \ (empty? \ t_1) \ (f_1 \ (first \ t_1) \ t_2 \ldots t_n))$$

with f_1 being a function of arity n and T being a table name.

We distinguish the two different transformation levels by the following sets and mappings: Let L_{DB} denote the set of DB expressions, L_{map} be the set of map expressions using the functions Id, Prj_i, Get_tuple, $Pred_i?$, and $Cjoin_i?$, and the operators L and K, and let L_λ be the set of λ-expressions. Then $\Sigma : L_{DB} \longrightarrow L_{map}$ defines the mapping from DB expressions to map expressions according to the definitions of the DB functions. $\Omega : L_{map} \longrightarrow L_\lambda$ translates map expressions into λ-expressions using the definitions for the different map operators.

4.2 Control Structure Manipulation and Functional Composition

The previous section introduced map expressions and λ-expressions to represent intermediate forms in the translation of DB expressions. This section describes two term rewriting systems to manipulate expressions in both forms. The first one manipulates control structures based on map expressions; the second one rewrites λ-expression to produce the final iterative programs. The first rewriting system is $(\mathcal{T}_{map}, \mathcal{R}_{map})$ where $\mathcal{R}_{map}$ contains the following rules:

Rule I:
$$((map* \; f_1 \; (map* \; f_2 \; str)) \longrightarrow (map* \; (L \; f_1 \; f_2) \; str))$$

Rule II:
$$((L \; f_1 \; (L \; f_2 \; f_3)) \longrightarrow (L \; (L \; f_1 \; f_2) \; f_3))$$

Rule III:
$$((L \; f_1 \; (map* \; f_2 \; str)) \longrightarrow (map* \; (L \; f_1 \; f_2) \; str))$$

The first rule implements vertical loop fusion using the operator L for functional combination. The second rule guarantees a canonical form for functional combination by grouping to the left. The last rule moves functions from the left over control structures, thus allowing further functional combination. Informally, the rule gives preference to functional combination over the application of functions to streams.

Theorem 4.1 $(\mathcal{T}_{map}, \mathcal{R}_{map})$ *is noetherian and confluent.*

Proof :

noetherian :

We use the following mapping from map expressions into $\mathcal{N}$:

$$\mu((map* \ f \ str)) \ = \ (\mu(f) + 2) * \mu(str)$$
$$\mu((L \ f_1 \ f_2)) \ \ \ = \ \mu(f_1) * (\mu(f_2) + 1)$$

then for all rules $(a \longrightarrow b)$, $\mu(a) > \mu(b)$ for all $\mu(a), \mu(b) > 1$.

confluence :

$\mathcal{R}_{map}$ induces the following critical pairs:

- Rule I superimposed on rule I:

    $$((map* \ f_1 \ (map* \ (L \ f_2 \ f_3) \ str)) \, , \ (map* \ (L \ f_1 \ f_2) \ (map* \ f_3 \ str)))$$

    The minimal form for the critical pair is:

    $$(map* \ (L \ f_1 \ (L \ f_2 \ f_3)) \ str)$$

- Rule II superimposed on rule II:

    $$((L \ f_1 \ (L \ (L \ f_2 \ f_3) \ f_4)) \, , \ (L \ (L \ f_1 \ f_2) \ (L \ f_3 \ f_4)))$$

    The minimal form for the critical pair is:

    $$(L \ (L \ (L \ f_1 \ f_2) \ f_3) \ f_4)$$

- Rule III superimposed on rule II:

    $$((L \ f_1 \ (map* \ (L \ f_2 \ f_3) \ str)) \, , \ (L \ (L \ f_1 \ f_2) \ (map* \ f_3 \ str)))$$

    The minimal form for the critical pair is:

    $$(map* \ (L \ (L \ f_1 \ f_2) \ f_3) \ str)$$

- Rule I superimposed on rule III:

    The same as the previous critical pair.

$\square$

The minimal form $t' = T_{map}(t)$ of any map expression t under $(T_{map}, \mathcal{R}_{map})$ reduces the number of $map*$ operators to the number of table variables used in the expression, thus later minimizing the number of loops necessary for evaluation.

Lemma 4.1 *For any map expression $m \in L_{map}$ the number of map* operators in the minimal form is equal to the number of table variables.*

Proof :

The only rule which removes *map** operators is rule I. We note that if $t = (map* \ f_1 \ (map* \ f_2 \ str))$ then the number of *map** operators in f_1 and f_2 is not changed when applying rule I to t. Since $(\mathcal{T}_{map}, \mathcal{R}_{map})$ is CR we choose a derivation which initially uses only rule I on expression:

$$(map* \ f_1 \ (map* \ \ldots (map* \ f_n \ str) \ldots))$$

for some n. By induction on n the expression reduces to

$$(map* \ (L \ (L \ldots (L \ f_1 \ f_2) \ldots f_{n-1}) \ f_n) \ str)$$

by applying rule I $n-1$ times. If f_i, $i = 1 \ldots n$ also contains expressions of the above form, the derivation continues the application of rule I. $\square$

Before presenting the next transformation system we give a small example using $(\mathcal{T}_{map}, \mathcal{R}_{map})$. Consider the DB expression:

```
(FILTER1
   (JOIN1
      (JOIN2 (FILTER2 (SCAN RR)) (PROJECT1 (SCAN SS)))
      (PROJECT2 (SCAN TT))))
```

with RR, SS, TT as table names. Mapping Σ translates the DB expression into the map expression

```
(map* pred1?
      (map* (map* (K Cjoin1?)
                  (map* Prj2 (map* Id TT)))
            (map* (map* (K Cjoin2?)
                        (map* Prj1 (map* Id SS)))
                  (map* Pred2? (map* Id RR)))))
```

and applying $(\mathcal{T}_{map}, \mathcal{R}_{map})$ yields the expression:

```
(map* (L (L f1 Pred2?) ID) RR)
```

where

```
f1 =  (map* (L (L (L f2 (K Cjoin2?)) Prj1) ID) SS)
```

and

```
f2 = (map* (L (L (L Pred1? (K Cjoin1?)) Prj2) Id) TT)
```

Note that the functions to the left of the $map*$ operators have been "pushed" into the innermost map expression by the last two rules. The innermost composition of functions (L (L (L Pred1? (K Cjoin1?)) Prj2) Id) represents a function of arity two whose second argument is bound to the innermost "map application" to table TT thus leaving a function of arity one. Its combination with (K Cjoin2?), Prj1, and ID yields a new function of arity two, whose arguments are successively bound to the two outermost tables together with the functional combination (L Pred2? ID).

The example shows the characteristic form of the final map expression in the case of nested $map*$'s. As $\mathcal{R}_{map}$ does not include rules to push functions into other map subexpressions from the right, $(\mathcal{T}_{map}, \mathcal{R}_{map})$ derives a minimal expression of the form:

$$(map* (L\ f_1\ f_2)\ table\_name)$$

with f_1 containing all other map subexpressions. f_2 represents either the function Id or a combination of basic functions which are applied to every element in the table before applying f_1.

The second transformation system $(\mathcal{T}_\lambda, \mathcal{R}_\lambda)$ is concerned with the manipulation of λ-expressions, more precisely with the transformation of expressions in the defined target language. The rewriting rules are quite similar to rules I, II and III in $(\mathcal{T}_P, \mathcal{R}_P)$. They generate expressions which evaluate conditions before evaluating functions as parameters for other functions. The set $\mathcal{R}_\lambda$ contains the following rules: Let f_1 be any function in $\mathcal{F}_1$, f_2 be any function in $\mathcal{F}_2$, and $t_1 \ldots t_n \in \mathcal{V}_P$ then

Rules Ia, Ib, Ic: function exchange rules

$$((f_1 \ (if \ t_1 \ t_2)) \longrightarrow (if \ t_1 \ (f_1 \ t_2)))$$

$$((f_2 \ (if \ t_1 \ t_2) \ t_3) \longrightarrow (if \ t_1 \ (f_2 \ t_2 \ t_3)))$$

$$((f_2 \ t_1 \ (if \ t_2 \ t_3)) \longrightarrow (if \ t_2 \ (f_2 \ f_1 \ t_3)))$$

Rule II: deletion rule

$$((if \ t_1 \ (\ldots (if \ t_1 \ t_2) \ldots)) \longrightarrow (if \ t_1 \ (\ldots t_2 \ldots)))$$

Rule III: distribution rule

$$((if \ (if \ t_1 \ t_2) \ t_3) \longrightarrow (if \ t_1 \ (if \ t_2 \ t_3)))$$

Rule IV: loop rule

$$((do \ (t_1 \ t_2 \ t_3) \ t_4 \ (if \ t_5 \ t_6)) \xrightarrow{C} (if \ t_5 \ (do \ (t_1 \ t_2 \ t_3) \ t_4 \ t_6)))$$

with condition $C = \sigma(t_1) \notin \mathcal{V}(\sigma(t_5))$, that is, the actual loop variable represented by t_1 does not occur as a variable in expression t_5.

Except for the last rule, all other rules in $\mathcal{R}_\lambda$ appear similarly in $\mathcal{R}_P$. Unfortunately, functional composition requires rule IV. The transformation into λ-expressions may create expressions with conditions whose evaluation does not depend on the loop at all. Consider the expression:

$$(map* \ (L \ (L \ (map* \ (L(K \ Cjoin1?) \ Id) \ SS) \ Pred1?) \ Id) \ RR)$$

which joins every element in RR satisfying the predicate $Pred1?$ with elements in SS. The corresponding λ-expression using $(\mathcal{T}_\lambda, \mathcal{R}_\lambda)$ without the rule IV results in

```
(do (t1 RR (rest t1))
    (empty? t1)
    (do (t2 SS (rest t2))
        (empty? t2)
        (if (pred1? (first t))
            (if (join1? (first t1) (first t2))
                (conc (first t1) (first t2))))))))
```

The inner loop is entered once for each element in SS before the evaluation of (if (pred1? (first t))...). The map expression clearly determines the independence of Pred1? from the inner loop. Applying the fourth rule we obtain the correct iterative program:

```
(do (t1 RR (rest t1))
    (empty? t1)
    (if (pred1? (first t))
        (do (t2 SS (rest t2))
            (empty? t2)
            (if (join1? (first t1) (first t2))
                (conc (first t1) (first t2)))))))
```

The fact that (T_λ, R_λ) has the desirable CR property follows from

Theorem 4.2 (T_λ, R_λ) *is noetherian and confluent.*

Sketch of the proof :

noetherian:

The mapping function ψ into $\mathcal{N}$ of lemma 3.1 may be extended to include loop expressions.

confluence:

The critical pairs created by the first five rules are similar to the ones for the proof in theorem 3.1. No additional critical pairs are induced by the loop rule. □

Using Ω for translating map expressions to λ-expressions and using the transformation system (T_λ, R_λ), we develop an algorithm which successively transforms map expressions into iterative programs of the target language. Let $t' = T R_\lambda(t)$ denote the result of applying (T_λ, R_λ) to expression t.

Algorithm $\mathcal{ML}$:

> **Input :** normalized map expression t **Output :** iterative expression

> *case*

>> If $t \in \{Id,\ Prj_i,\ Get\_tuple,\ Pred_i?,\ \text{and}\ Cjoin_i?\}$:

>>> return $(\Omega(t))$;

>> If $t = (K\ f)$:

>>> return $(\mathcal{AP}(\Omega(K),\ \Omega(f)))$;

>> If $t = (L\ f_1\ f_2)$:

>>> $t_1 := \mathcal{ML}(f_1);\ t_2 := \mathcal{ML}(f_2)$;
>>> return$(\mathcal{TR}_\lambda(\mathcal{AP}(\Omega(L),\ t_1,\ t_2)))$;

>> If $t = (map*\ f_1\ str)$:

>>> $t_1 := \mathcal{ML}(f_1)$;
>>> return $(\mathcal{TR}_\lambda(\mathcal{AP}(\Omega(map*),\ t_1,\ str)))$;

> *end_case;*

Algorithm $\mathcal{ML}$ recursively combines functions and control structure information according to operators K, L, and $map*$, and simplifies their combination using $\mathcal{TR}_\lambda$. The input to $\mathcal{ML}$ must be in canonical form, otherwise the algorithm does not perform its translation correctly.

4.3   The Transformation Algorithm

While the last section developed the transformation of map expressions into λ-expressions, this section presents the complete transformation algorithm to translate DB expressions into iterative programs. The algorithm calls function *Make_result* which moves the variable *result* and function *out* into the final expression. *Make_result* is best described by the following two rules which are applied repetitively to conditional expressions and loop statements:

$$((set\ result\ (out\ (if\ t_1\ t_2)\ result)) \longrightarrow$$
$$(if\ t_1\ (set\ result\ (out\ t_2\ result)))))$$
$$((set\ result\ (out\ (do\ t_1\ t_2\ t_3)\ result)) \longrightarrow$$
$$(do\ t_1\ t_2\ (set\ result\ (out\ t_3\ result)))))$$

Both rules push the assignment statement together with function *out* over conditional expressions and loop statements down to function expressions which compute the resulting tuples.

ALGORITHM $T\mathcal{R}_{map}$:

Input : QEP qep   **Output** : iterative expression

begin

$\quad t_1 := \Phi(qep);\qquad$ /* *translate qep into DB expression* */
$\quad t_2 := T_{map}(\Sigma(t_1));$ /* *transform map expressions* */
$\quad t_3 := \mathcal{ML}(t_2);\qquad$ /* *transform λ - expressions* */
/* create assignment statements */

$\quad t_4 := (set\ result\ (out\ prg\ result))\ [prg\ /\ t_3];$
$\quad t_5 := Make\_result(t_4);$
$\quad t_6 := ((set\ result\ *empty*)\ prg)\ [prg\ /\ t_5];$

end

Theorem 4.3 *Given a QEP qep accessing n tables, algorithm $T\mathcal{R}_{map}$ produces an iterative expression with n loops.*

Sketch of proof :

Termination follows from $(T_{map}, \mathcal{R}_{map})$ and $(T_\lambda, \mathcal{R}_\lambda)$ being noetherian, and the termination of $\mathcal{ML}$. The termination of $\mathcal{ML}$ is guaranteed by $(T_\lambda, \mathcal{R}_\lambda)$ being noetherian and by the decreasing numbers of functions which are combined with each recursive call. The number of loops in the final output is determined by the number of *map*$*$ operators. By lemma 4.1 the number of *map*$*$'s in the minimal expression is equal to the number of tables, thus leading to an iterative program of n loops. $\square$

To estimate the running time of algorithm $\mathcal{TR}_{map}$, let the initial QEP consist of n actions and m tables. For any well formed QEP $n \geq m$. The initial map expression contains $n + m - 1$ $map*$ operators with n functions as their first arguments. Transformation system $(\mathcal{T}_{map}, \mathcal{R}_{map})$ applies its first rule $n - 1$ times, the second rule at most n times and the last rule at most $n*m$ times. The resulting time complexity is $O(n^2)$. The minimal form consists of at most $n + m$ L operators, m K operators, and exactly m $map*$ operators. In algorithm $\mathcal{ML}$ the application $\mathcal{AP}$ of λ-expressions for operators L and K takes constant time. In each combination each rule of $(\mathcal{T}_\lambda, \mathcal{R}_\lambda)$ is applied at most n times, so $\mathcal{ML}$ has a time complexity of $O(n^2)$. Since the number of translations between the different expressions is linear in the number of operators, the overall complexity is $O(n^2)$.

Example 5

Using the DB expression of example 3 on page 23, transformation algorithm $\mathcal{TR}_{map}$ derives the canonical form

```
(map*
  (L (L (map* (L (L (L Prj1   (K Cjoin1?)) Pred1?) Id)
              PAPERS)
         (get EMP)) Id)
  (access_index pred0? ISTAT))
```

where

Pred0?	denotes $\lambda\, t_1.(\text{pred0? } t_1)$
Pred1?	denotes $\lambda\, t_1.(\text{pred1? } t_1)$
Cjoin1?	denotes $\lambda\, t_1.\lambda t_2.((\text{if join1? } t_1\, t_2)\, (\text{conc } t_1\, t_2))$
Prj1	denotes $\lambda\, t_1.(\text{prj1 } t_1)$
Id	denotes the identity function

and

pred0?	implements the predicate	$(\text{Status} = PROF)$
pred1?	implements the predicate	$(\text{Year} > 1980)$
join1?	implements the predicate	$(\text{Emp\#} = \text{Emp\#})$
prj1	implements the projection list	(Name)

The transformation step $\mathcal{ML}$ produces the iterative program

```
(DO (str1 (access_index pred0? ISTAT) (rest str1))
    (empty? str1)
    (DO (str2 PAPERS (rest str2))
        (empty? str2)
        (if (pred1? (first str2))
            (if (join1? (get_tuple EMP (first str1))
                        (first str2))
                (out (prj1 (conc (get_tuple EMP (first str))
                                 (first str2))) result)))))
```

before the function *Make_result* generates the final iterative form

```
((set result *empty*)
 (DO (str1 (access_index pred0? ISTAT) (rest str1))
     (empty? str1)
     (DO (str2 PAPERS (rest str2))
         (empty? str2)
         (if (pred1? (first str2))
             (if (join1? (get_tuple EMP (first str1))
                         (first str2))
                 (set result
                     (out (prj1 (conc (get_tuple EMP (first str))
                                      (first str2))) result)))))))
```

Notice that algorithm $\mathcal{TR}_{map}$ produces the same program as algorithm $\mathcal{TR}_R$. □

4.4   Extending Query Evaluation Plans to Query Programs

In Section 3.6 we discussed the extension of the recursion based transformation
to horizontal loop fusion. The example provided there indicates the difficulties
encountered when including this kind of transformation into algorithm $\mathcal{TR}_R$.
We investigate the same extension for the two-level approach described in this
chapter. We show how horizontal loop fusion is naturally embedded into the

second transformation algorithm. Furthermore, we briefly discuss the extension of QEPs to *query programs* to evaluate more than one query at a time. The transformation combines several queries, if possible, to generate one iterative program which avoids repeated access to the same tables.

Consider the example of Section 3.6. There we translated the DB expression (union (filter1 (scan RR)) (filter2 (scan RR))) into an iterative program. With some user guidance and a new definition for the union operator the generated program consisted of one loop. We notice that the union operator does not perform any functional transformation on elements of the input streams. Similar to the concatenation of elements to streams, we introduce $\ll str_1\ str_2 \gg$ to denote the concatenation, or union, of streams in map expressions. For the notation $\ll\gg$ we use the following two transformation rules:

$$r_1 = (\ll (map* \ f_1 \ str) \ (map* \ f_2 \ str) \gg \longrightarrow (map* \ \ll f_1 \ f_2 \gg \ str))$$
$$r_2 = (\ll (L \ f_1 \ f_2) \ (L \ f_3 \ f_2) \gg \longrightarrow (L \ \ll f_1 \ f_3 \gg \ f_2))$$

The first rule implements horizontal loop fusion. The second rule allows the distribution of $\ll \gg$ over the L operator combining the first operands if the second operands are the same. These rules are either applied after the transformation by $(\mathcal{T}_{map}, \mathcal{R}_{map})$ or they may safely be included into $\mathcal{R}_{map}$ as the following lemma shows.

Lemma 4.2 $\mathcal{R}'_{map} = (L_{map}, \mathcal{R}_{map} \cup \{r_1, r_2\})$ *is noetherian and confluent.*

Proof :

noetherian:

We define $\mu(\ll \ str_1 \ str_2 \ \gg) = 2^{\mu(str_1)+\mu(str_2)}$. The mapping for $\ll\gg$ guarantees $\mu(a) > \mu(b)$ for all rules $(a \longrightarrow b)$.

confluence:

In addition to the critical pairs derived in the proof for theorem 4.1 there exist the following new critical pairs which are induced by r_1 and r_2.

Rule I superimposed on r_1:

$$(\ll (map* \ (L \ f_1 \ f_2) \ str) \ (map* \ (L \ f_3 \ f_2) \ str) \gg,$$
$$(map* \ \ll f_1 \ f_3 \gg \ (map* \ f_2 \ str)))$$

Rule II superimposed on r_2:

$$(\ll (L\ (L\ f_1\ f_2)\ f_3)\ (L\ (L\ f_4\ f_2)\ f_3) \gg,\ (L\ \ll f_1\ f_4 \gg (L\ f_2\ f_3)))$$

Rule III superimposed on r_2:

$$(\ll (map*\ (L\ f_1\ f_2)\ str)\ \ (map*\ (L\ f_4\ f_2)\ str) \gg,$$
$$(L\ \ll f_1\ f_4 \gg (map*\ f_2\ str)))$$

The normal forms of all three critical pairs are the same under $\mathcal{R}_{map}\ \cup\ \{r_1, r_2\}$. $\square$

If we translate the above DB expression into a map expression and apply the set of rules $\mathcal{R}'_{map} = \mathcal{R}_{map} \cup \{r_1, r_2\}$, the example yields the normal form

$$(map*\ (L\ \ll Pred_1?\ Pred_2? \gg Id)\ RR).$$

For the translation into the target language the expression $\ll f_1\ f_2 \gg$ simply maps into a *sequence* of expressions. Therefore the above map expression translates into the program:[2]

```
((set result *empty*)
 (do (t1 RR (rest t1))
     (empty? t1)
     ((if (pred1? (first t1))
          (set result (out (first t1) result)))
      (if (pred2? (first t1))
          (set result (out (first t1) result)))))))
```

Notice that the generated program is different from the one derived in Section 3.6; however, they are computationally equivalent.

Finally, the optimization by horizontal loop fusion can also improve the evaluation of a *set of QEPs*, called a *query program*. Consider the two QEPs (project1 (scan RR)) and (filter2 (scan RR)) which access the *same* table RR. Instead of generating programs which evaluate each QEP independently, we may evaluate them by *one program*. For this purpose we introduce the new combinator $\langle\rangle$ with exactly the same transformation rules as for $\ll\gg$. The example then transforms into

---

[2]In practice, there are some more changes necessary in the transformation system $T\mathcal{R}_\lambda$ to obtain this iterative program.

$$(map* (L \langle Prj_1? \ Pred_2? \rangle \ Id) \ RR).$$

For the translation into the target language we generate different result variables depending on the number of combined QEPs. For the example the translation yields the iterative program

```
((set result1 *empty*)
 (set result2 *empty*)
 (do (t1 RR (rest t1))
     (empty? t1)
     ((set result1 (out (first t1) result1))
      (if (pred2? (first t1))
          (set result2 (out (first t1) result2))))))
```

Clearly, since both QEPs access the same table, their combination into one program decreases the total number of necessary table scans.

4.5 Comparison of Algorithms

This section compares the two transformation algorithms TR_R and TR_{map} developed in this and in the previous chapter. We discuss their strength and weaknesses and show how they supplement each other despite their differences.

So far we have carefully avoided the question of whether or not both transformation algorithms generate the same programs. Theorems 3.4 and 4.3 guarantee that programs generated from the same QEP contain the same number of loops. Since the transformations performed by both algorithms are sound, the generated programs are computationally equivalent. They are also syntactically identical. However, to prove the latter is more difficult since the transformations proceed differently. The examples provided for both transformations strongly suggest that the resulting programs are indeed the same. Instead of making a laborious effort for proving syntactic equivalence we prefer to compare both transformation algorithms more informally and point out differences which make it cumbersome to translate recursive expressions to map expressions or λ-expressions.

One of the major differences is the kind of intermediate results we obtain during the transformation process. The recursion based transformation algorithm $\mathcal{TR}_R$ always derives expressions whose evaluation leads to constant streams. Map subexpressions may result in function streams, making it necessary to keep track of the list of unbound variables during the transformation into the target language. For this reason we also have to introduce the auxiliary operator K to guarantee the correct order of variable bindings.

This observation is closely related to two other major differences. First, to obtain expressions which always yield constant streams, algorithm $\mathcal{TR}_R$ alternates between the manipulation of recursive expressions and the generation of loops. On the other hand, the transformation of map expressions is completed first before any translation into iterative expressions is performed. Second, the normal form of map expressions encourages a "bottom up" or "innermost first" translation into iterative programs. Algorithm $\mathcal{TR}_{map}$ produces the innermost loop of the iterative program first, the outermost loop last. On the other hand the recursion based transformation generates programs "top down": To produce the outermost loop first the computation of the ideal form reverses the functional order by unfolding, simplification and folding. The alternation of unfolding and folding is performed repetitively without much progress in the overall transformation. The separation of control structure information and functional composition in map expressions avoids these time consuming steps. Intermediate stream are eliminated using only one rule. The functional combination is delayed until the final iterative programs are generated. Much effort is needed to correctly perform functional combination; we must introduce λ-expressions. In the recursion based transformation the use of stream operators implemented functional combination elegantly and without additional overhead.

A major problem for a formal translation between map and recursive expression arises from the use of partial functions in map expressions which we introduced to simplify the transformation into iterative programs. For a possible translation into recursive programs we need to extend them to total functions. For example the λ-expression $\lambda\, t_1.(if(pred?\ t_1)\ t_1)$ has to be redefined as $\lambda\, t_1.(if(pred?\ t_1)\ t_1\ \bot)$ where $\bot$ denotes the "empty element". This change implies new transformation rules for functional combination, such as $((out \perp str) \longrightarrow str)$, to generate the recursive programs.

The previous section and Section 3.6 extended both transformation approaches to include horizontal loop fusion. In the recursion based approach a major effort is necessary to include this kind of improvement. From the derivation in Section 3.6 it seems to be doubtful if such a transformation is possible without some user guidance [BD77]. For map expressions however, we easily extended the transformation algorithm to naturally include this optimization.

Chapter 5

The Transformation of Aggregate Functions

Many database systems, such as SYSTEM R and INGRES, permit the computation of counts, sums, averages and other aggregate quantities [A*76] [SW*76]. Aggregation is usually performed over a set of tuples yielding a singleton value. We can also *partition*, or group, tuples into subsets according to common values of one or more attributes; then aggregation is performed for each of the subsets yielding a set of singleton values. Consider the QUEL-query

```
Range e is EMP
Retrieve (Department_Salary = Sum(e.Sal by e.Dept))
```

on relation EMP [SW*76]. This query computes the sum of salaries for each department in the EMP relation. As the number of departments is not known in advance, one possible evaluation strategy is to *sort* the relation EMP on department values before the salary sum for each department is computed.

This processing strategy is not optimal. Klug noticed that in many cases the aggregate computation — or at least part of it — may be performed while sorting [Klu82]. For instance, in the above example, whenever two tuples are compared and they agree in their department value we can merge them into a *new tuple* by adding their salaries. Applying this improvement throughout the sort, the final result contains a sorted list of tuples with *exactly one tuple* for each department recording its salary. An additional scan of the sorted relation to perform aggregation becomes unnecessary. A primary gain in execution speed

79

results from the sort step since the number of tuples decreases while sorting. Klug suggested a specially designed set of access functions which implement the combination of sorting and aggregate computation [Klu82]. [BD83] uses the same idea for the elimination of duplicate tuples in relations.

In this chapter we derive these improvements for aggregate functions by the methods of functional programming and program transformation. We show how to generate these efficient programs from initial specifications which independently define the aggregate functions and the sorting algorithm. Their transformation is based on ideas developed in the previous two chapters. First, for the manipulation of control structure information we use map expressions extended by an additional operator, called *tree*, to express more complex control structures. We present two different transformation schemes for the tree operator's translation into iteration. Second, we use recursion based transformation to derive completely new functions from existing ones. We introduce a new transformation step, called *abstraction*, which defines new functions for commonly used subexpressions.

To be more concrete about the performed transformations, we fix some of the functions and algorithms. To implement sorting we use the *sort-merge* algorithm [Knu73]. We demonstrate many transformation steps on aggregation using the aggregate function *sum*. We shall show how the proposed transformation generalizes to other aggregate functions as well.

In contrast to the transformation algorithms presented in the previous two chapters, several transformation steps in the following sections are non-trivial, thus needing some user guidance to yield the desired transformation result. The transformation is independent of any particular aggregate function performed. Therefore we view the recursion based transformation as a *proof for the soundness of rules* which manipulate map expressions.

Our approach has two main benefits. First, independently defined functions for sorting and aggregation permit the design of a modular interface for QEPs.[1] They relieve the optimizer of making these improvements. Second, the transformation is effective even if the aggregate function is not known in ad-

---

[1]Compare Section 2.1, which defines QEPs.

vance. The transformation system can try to combine a user provided function with internally defined processing strategies to generate more efficient programs for its evaluation.

5.1 Basic Definitions

This section introduces some definitions techniques used later in this chapter. Our interest focuses on aggregate functions whose results are determined on *subsets of relations*, which produce a stream of values, one value for each subset. To evaluate an aggregate, the database system first sorts the relation on values of some attribute(s) A that determine the subsets. Sorting introduces *ordered streams*; we only consider streams whose values occur in increasing order based on some attribute values(s) A, i.e.

$$(\texttt{first str}) \leq_A (\texttt{first (rest str)})$$

where $\leq_A$ is a total ordering on A. If the condition holds for all elements of the stream then we say the stream is *ordered* and write $(ordered_A\ str)$.

For implementing sorting we use the *sort-merge* algorithm [Knu73]. The algorithm performs sorting as follows. In the first phase the stream of tuples is divided into several streams of equal length called *runs*. Each run is sorted before beginning the second phase, the *merge phase*. The merge starts with pairs of sorted runs that are merged into one sorted run. Each subsequent phase merges pairs of runs produced by the previous phase into a sorted run twice as long as the input runs. We define the merge function in linear recursive form as follows:

```
(merge str1 str2) =
(if (empty? str1) str2
    (if (empty? str2) str1
        (if (gr? (first str1) (first str2))
            (out (first str2) (merge str1 (rest str2)))
            (if (eq? (first str1) (first str2))
                (out (first str2) (merge str1 (rest str2)))
                (out (first str1) (merge (rest str1) str2)))))))
```

81

We assume that predicates **gr?** and **eq?** correctly implement the comparison of *greater* and *equal* on some attribute A. In most cases the particular attribute is irrelevant for the transformation; we use $eq_A?$, $gr_A?$, and $merge_A$ whenever necessary to avoid confusion.

For a complete specification of the sort-merge algorithm we introduce another *control structure* operator, called *tree*, which was initially defined by Williams [Wil82]. For its definition we define the operators lf and rg with

$$(lf\ str) = <e_1 \ldots e_{half}>, \qquad (rg\ str) = <e_{half+1} \ldots e_n>$$

where *str* is a stream, n its length, and

$$half = \begin{cases} \lceil n/2 \rceil & if \quad even(\lceil n/2 \rceil) \\ \lceil n/2 \rceil + 1 & if \quad odd(\lceil n/2 \rceil) \end{cases}$$

Both operators are treated as base functions which split streams into a *left* and a *right* part of (almost) equal length. The following properties hold for lf, rg, and *union*:

$$(union\ (lf\ str)\ (rg\ str)) \ = \ str$$
$$(union\ (map*\ f\ (lf\ str))\ (map*\ f\ (rg\ str))) \ = \ (map*\ f\ str)$$

Additionally, we define the *height* of the stream *str* by:

$$(height\ str) = \lceil log(n) \rceil \text{ with } n = (length\ str)$$

We are now ready to define the operator *tree*. Like *map**, *tree* takes two arguments, a function f of arity two and a stream of elements *str*:

$$(tree\ f\ str) = \begin{cases} str\ if\ (length\ str) = 1 \\ (f\ (tree\ f\ (lf\ str))\ (tree\ f\ (rg\ str))) \end{cases}$$

Williams observes that the operator *tree* expresses concurrency inherent in some algorithms [Wil82]. For example, the summation of a list of integers, *str*, may be evaluated by $(tree\ +\ str)$.

As the sort-merge algorithm is based on merging *runs*, i.e. ordered streams of equal length, we introduce the operator *conv_str* to split a stream of elements into a *stream of stream of elements*. Using the operators *tree* and *conv_str* we define the function *merge_sort*:

$$(merge\_sort \; str) = (tree \; merge \; (map* \; sort \; (conv\_str \; str)))$$

where $(sort \; str) = (tree \; merge \; str)$.

$(map* \; sort \; (conv\_str \; str))$ returns a stream of ordered streams as the initial runs. Whenever *merge* is applied to two ordered streams the result is an ordered stream consisting of elements from both inputs. The "tree-like" application of *merge* ultimately returns an ordered stream of elements.

For the aggregation we introduce the function $sum\_by_{B,A}$ which, for the set of tuples with the same attribute A value, computes the sum of attribute values B. To compute the correct result, $sum\_by_{B,A}$ expects a stream ordered on A as its input. Generally, we use the notation sum_by instead of $sum\_by_{B,A}$:

```
(sum_by str)  = (if (empty str) *empty*
                    (sum (first str) (rest str)))


(sum ele str) = (if (empty? str)
                    (out ele str)
                    (if (eq? ele (first str))
                        (sum (add ele (first str))
                             (rest str))
                        (out ele
                             (sum (first str) (rest str)))))
```

We assume **add** to be a function which adds the values of two tuples and creates a new tuple by $(add \; e_1 \; e_2) = < b_1 + b_2, a_1 >$ with $e_i = < b_i, a_i >$.

5.2 The Transformation of Merge and Sum

This section describes the transformation of (sum_by (merge_sort str)) which we carry out on two different levels. First, using the tree notation we perform *structural manipulation* showing how to intertwine $sort\_merge_A$ and $sum\_by_{B,A}$. This step yields the specification of a program which executes the aggregate function while sorting. Although the tree notation is well suited for transformation, its recursive nature does not guarantee an efficient execution. For this reason we develop two different transformation schemes to replace "tree recursion" by extended linear recursion and then by iteration. The programs derived by the two schemes differ in their computational behavior. While the first one maintains a tree-structured computation, the second one resembles a left linear computation tree. As we shall see, both translation schemes have advantages.

The second transformation level addresses the functional combination of merge and sum_by. We use their recursive definition to transform both functions into a new function *sum_merge* via a set of rules similar to set $\mathcal{R}_P$ of Chapter 3. This step needs further user guidance to achieve the desired transformation goal.

5.2.1 Structural Transformation

As a first step of the structural transformation, we provide a sufficient condition for distributing a function f over the *tree* operator. In the proof we again use of the interchangeability of singleton elements and streams of one element.

Theorem 5.1 *Let f_1 and f_2 be two functions. If*

$$(f_1 \, (f_2 \, str_1 \, str_2)) = (f_1 \, (f_2 \, (f_1 \, str_1) \, (f_1 \, str_2)))$$

then

$$(f_1 \, (tree \, f_2 \, str)) = (tree \, (L \, f_1 \, f_2) \, (map* \, f_1 \, str)).$$

Proof :

The proof is by induction on the height h of stream str:

If $h = 0$, then

$$(f_1 \, (tree \, f_2 \, str)) = (f_1 \, str)$$
$$(tree \, (L \, f_1 \, f_2) \, (map* \, f_1 \, str)) \; = \; (f_1 \, str)$$

Suppose the theorem holds for $h = i$, then let $h = i + 1$:

$$(f_1 \, (tree \, f_2 \, str)) =$$

by the definition of tree

$$(f_1 \, (f_2 \, (tree \, f_2 \, (lf \, str)) \, (tree \, f_2 \, (rg \, str))))$$

84

by assumption of theorem

$$(f_1 \, (f_2 \, (f_1 \, (tree \, f_2 \, (lf \, str))) \, (f_1 \, (tree \, f_2 \, (rg \, str)))))$$

by induction hypothesis

$$(f_1 \, (f_2 \quad (tree \, (L \, f_1 \, f_2) \, (map* \, f_1 \, (lf \, str)))$$
$$(tree \, (L \, f_1 \, f_2) \, (map* \, f_1 \, (rg \, str)))))$$

definition of L and definition of $tree$

$$(tree \, (L \, f_1 \, f_2) \, (map* \, f_1 \, str))$$

□

The condition on f_1 and f_2 in the theorem is quite strict. Most functions are not as "well behaved" as required. Intuitively, the theorem requires f_1 and f_2 to be almost independent to allow the partial computation by f_2 before the application of f_1. However, the computation of both functions is not completely independent. Their order of application cannot be exchanged. To apply theorem 5.1 to $(sum\_by_{B,A} \, (tree \, merge_A \, (map* \, sort_A \, (conv\_str \, str))))$ we need to show that both functions satisfy the condition of the theorem. We describe their computational results in terms of their inputs using $multisets$ [DM79].

1. $str = (merge_A \, str_1 \, str_2)$

   (a) $(ordered_A \, str_1) \wedge (ordered_A \, str_2) \implies (ordered_A \, str)$

   (b) $str = str_1 \cup str_2$ where $(length \, str) = (length \, str_1) + (length \, str_2)$

2. $str = (sum\_by_{B,A} \, str_1)$

   (a) $(ordered_A \, str_1) \implies (ordered_A \, str)$

   (b) $(ordered_A \, str_1) \implies$

   $$str = \{t : \, t.B = \Sigma\{t_i.B : \, t_i.A = \, t.a \wedge t_i \in str_1\}\}$$

   (c) $(ordered_A \, str_1) \implies \forall \, t_1, t_2 \in str : t_1.A \neq t_2.A$

Based on the descriptions of the operators we show that

$$(sum\_by_{B,A} \, (merge_A \, str_1 \, str_2)) =$$

85

$$(sum\_by_{B,A} \ (merge_A \ (sum\_by_{B,A} \ str_1) \ (sum\_by_{B,A} \ str_2)))$$

3. $str = (sum\_by_{B,A} \ (merge_A \ str_1 \ str_2))$

    (a) $(ordered_A \ str_1) \land (ordered_A \ str_2) \implies (ordered_A \ str)$

        follows from 1a and 2a.

    (b) $(ordered_A \ str_1) \land (ordered_A \ str_2) \implies$
$$str = \{t : \ t.B = \textstyle\sum \{t_i.B : \ (t_i.A = t.A) \land (t_i \in str_1 \ \cup \ str_2)\}\}$$

        follows from 1b and 2b.

    (c) $(ordered_A \ str_1) \land (ordered_A \ str_2) \implies \forall t_1, t_2 \in str : \ t_1.A \neq t_2.A$

        follows from 1a and 2c.

4. $str' = (merge_A \ (sum\_by_{B,A} \ str_1) \ (sum\_by_{B,A} \ str_2))$

    (a) $(ordered_A \ str_1) \land (ordered_A \ str_2) \implies (ordered_A \ str')$

        follows from 1a and 2a.

    (b)
$$\begin{aligned} str' = \ &\{t : t.B = \textstyle\sum\{t_i.B : \ (t_i.A = t.A) \land (t_i \in str_1)\}\} \ \cup \\ &\{t : t.B = \textstyle\sum\{t_i.B : \ (t_i.A = t.A) \land (t_i \in str_2)\}\} \end{aligned}$$

        follows from 1b and 2b.

5. $str'' = (sum\_by_{B,A} \ str')$

    (a) $(ordered_A \ str_1) \land (ordered_A \ str_2) \implies (ordered_A \ str'')$

        follows from 2a and 4a.

    (b) $(ordered_A \ str_1) \land (ordered_A \ str_2) \implies$
$$str'' = \{t : \ t.B = \textstyle\sum \{t_i.B : \ (t_i.A = t.A) \land (t_i \in str_1 \ \cup \ str_2)\}\}$$

        follows from the definition of str' in 4b, and the definition of $\textstyle\sum$.

    (c) $(ordered_A \ str_1) \land (ordered_A \ str_2) \implies \forall t_1, t_2 \in str'' : \ t_1.A \neq t_2.A$

        follows from 2c and 4a.

Since 3a, 3b, and 3c are the same as 5a, 5b and 5c we can apply theorem 5.1 twice as follows:

$$(sum\_by_{B,A} \ (tree \ merge_A \ (map* \ sort_A \ (conv\_str \ str))))) =$$
$$(tree \ (L \ sum\_by_{B,A} \ merge_A)$$

$$(map* \ sum\_by_{B,A} \ (map* \ sort_A \ (conv\_str \ str)))))$$

Using the rule $((map* \ f_1 \ (map* \ f_2 \ str)) \longrightarrow (map* \ (L \ f_1 \ f_2) \ str))$ we obtain

$$(tree \ (L \ sum\_by_{B,A} \ merge_A) \ (map* \ (L \ sum\_by_{B,A} \ sort_A) \ (conv\_str \ str))))$$

By the definition of L and $sort_A$ we rewrite $(L \ sum\_by_{B,A} \ sort_A)$ as

$$(sum\_by_{B,A} \ (tree \ merge_A \ str))$$
$$= \ (tree \ (L \ sum\_by_{B,A} \ merge_A) \ (map* \ sum\_by_{B,A} \ str))$$
$$= \ (tree \ (L \ sum\_by_{B,A} \ merge_A) \ str)$$

since the application of $sum\_by_{B,A}$ to each element of the stream str is superfluous. From this derivation follows

Theorem 5.2 $(sum\_by_{B,A} \ (tree \ merge_A \ (map* \ sort_A \ (conv\_str \ str))))) =$

$$(tree \ (L \ sum\_by_{B,A} \ merge_A) \ (map* \ sum\_sort_A \ (conv\_str \ str))))$$

where $(sum\_sort_A \ str) = (tree \ (L \ sum\_by_{B,A} \ merge_A) \ str)$.

The next section investigates further transformations of the expression (sum_by (merge str1 str2)) based on the recursive definition of both functions. The rest of this section develops two different transformation schemes to replace the *tree* operator by extended linear recursive functions. Although both translations correctly implement the *tree* operator, their computational behavior is quite different. We discuss this difference in more detail after we have presented both transformations. Instead of the *tree* operator we use a more general notation to describe the translation and later apply the result to our more special case. For reasons of clarity we assume the stream str to contain at least one element. The following definitions and proofs can be easily extended for the empty stream. Let

```
(f str)  = (if (eq? (length str) 1) str
              (f1 (f (1f str) (f rg str)))))
```

```
(f' str) = (if (eq? (length str) 1) str
               (f' (g str)))


(g str)  = (if (empty? str) *empty*
               (out (f1 (first str) (first (rest str)))
                    (g (rest (rest str)))))
```

Clearly, f' is extended linear recursive and g is linear recursive. To show that

$$(f\ str) = (f'\ str)$$

we specify necessary properties. We assume f1 is an associative function with a left and right identity i_{f_1}. The identity i_{f_1} is used implicitly whenever (first (rest str)) is undefined, i.e. the stream str contains only one element.

Proposition 5.1
If (height str) $= n$, $n > 0$, *then* (height (g str)) $= n - 1$.

The proof follows from the definition of g.

Proposition 5.2
If (height str) > 1 *then* (g str) = (union (g (lf str)) (g (rg str)))

Lemma 5.1 (f' (g str)) = (g (union (f' (lf str)) (f' (rg str))))

Proof :
The proof is by induction on the (height str)

If (height str) $= 0$, then (length str) $= 1$

```
(f' (g str)) = str
(g (union (f' (lf str)) (f' (rg str)))) =
(g (union *empty* str)) = str
```

If (height str) $= 1$, then

88

```
        (f' (g str))
      = (f1 (first str) (first (rest str)))
      = (g str)
      = (g (union (f' (lf str)) (f' (rg str))))
```

Suppose the lemma holds for (height str)$= i$, then for (height str)$= i + 1$ we have

```
        (f' (g str))
        by definition of f'
      = (f' (g (g str)))
        (height (g (g str))) = i - 1
      = (g (union (f' (lf (g str))) (f' (rg (g str)))))
        by proposition 5.2
      = (g (union (f' (g (lf str))) (f' (g (rg str)))))
        by definition of f'
      = (g (union (f' (lf str)) (f' (rg str))))
```

$\Box$

Lemma 5.1 enables us to prove

Theorem 5.3 (f str) = (f' str)

Proof :

The proof is by induction on (height str).

If (height)$= 0$, then

```
        (f str) = str = (f' str)
```

If the theorem holds for (height)$= i$, let (height str)$= i + 1$, then

```
        (f str)
        by definition of f
      = (f1 (f (lf str)) (f (rg str)))
        by induction hypothesis
      = (f1 (f' (lf str)) (f' (rg str)))
```

by definition of **g**

= (g (union (f' (lf str)) (f' (rg str)))))

by lemma 5.1

= (f' (g str))

by definition of **f'**

= (f' str))

☐

Theorem 5.3 allows us to replace the nonlinear function **f** by the two re-cursive functions **f'** and **g**. Furthermore, **f'** and **g** can be transformed into a single iterative program consisting of two nested loops. If we define ($tree\ f_1\ str$) = (**f** str) the transformation applies immediately to the operator $tree$. Let f_1 be the $merge$ function. Clearly, its right identity is the empty stream. $merge$ is also associative, i.e. any order of $merge$ operations returns an ordered stream. The iterative version resembles the sort-merge program which computes its in-termediate results in rounds [BD83]. In each round two streams of equal length are merged into one. The computation in rounds actually simulates the initial $tree$ specification in a bottom up manner.

In contrast to the first transformation the second leads to a computation which resembles a left linear computation tree. The transformation is partially due to M. Wand whose motivation is the same as ours, i.e. the elimination of recursion [Wan80]. However, his desire to minimize the manipulation of the runtime stack leads to a solution whose computational behavior is completely different from the initial recursive program. We begin the transformation by defining function **g1** as (g1 str res) = (f1 res (f str)), then

```
    (g1 str res)
     by definition of f
=   (f1 res (f1 (f (lf str)) (f (rg str))))
     associativity of f1
=   (f1 (f1 res (f (lf str))) (f (rg str)))
     by definition of g1
=   (f1 (g1 (lf str) res) (f (rg str)))
     by definition of g1
=   (g1 (rg str) (g1 (lf str) res))
```

Thus we can replace f by

```
(g1 str res) = (if (= (length str) 1)
                   (f1 res (first str))
                   (g1 (rg str) (g1 (lf str) res)))
```

with $(f\ str) = (g1\ str\ i_{f_1})$.

As g1 is still a nonlinear recursive function we have to replace it by another function g2. Due to simplified assumptions about the stream str we depart from Wand's transformation and introduce

```
(g2 str res) = (if (= (length str) 1)
                   (f1 res (first str))
                   (g2 (rest str) (f1 res (first str))))
```

We assume (g2 *empty* res) = res.

Proposition 5.3
If str = (union str1 str2) *then*

```
(g2 str res) = (g2 str2 (g2 str1 res))
```

Using proposition 5.3 we prove

Theorem 5.4 (g1 str res) = (g2 str res)

Proof :

The proof is by induction on (height str).

If (height str)$= 0$, then

$$\text{(g1 str res)} = \text{(f1 res (first str))} = \text{(g2 str res)}$$

If the theorem holds for (height str)$= i$, let (height str)$= i + 1$, then

```
      (g1 str res)
      by definition of g1
  =   (g1 (rg str) (g1 (lf str) res))
      by hypothesis
  =   (g2 (rg str) (g2 (lf str) res))
      by proposition 5.3
  =   (g2 str res)
```

□

From theorem 5.4 we conclude (g2 str i_{f_1}) = (g1 str i_{f_1}) = (f str)
The form of g2 immediately leads to a more complete definition of a function
g2' which includes the empty stream:

```
(g2' str res) =
    (if (empty? str) res
        (g2' (rest str) (f1 res (first str)))))
```

The tail recursive form of the definition leads to in an iterative program [Coh80].

If f1 is the *merge* function and *str* is a stream of ordered streams, then
g2' successively merges each element of the stream with res, the *accumulation*
of streams so far [Bir84]. As the length of res increases with every call to g2'
we obtain an n^2 algorithm. Clearly, the transformation has changed the $n\ log n$
complexity of the initial specification.

Despite its disadvantage in the example, there may exist cases where one
would favor the latter translation. To justify our claim, we examine in more detail
the representation of tuples streams and tables in database systems. Usually,
tuples in tables are stored on secondary storage. For the evaluation of queries

the database system needs to access tables in *memory* to perform the necessary operations. For this purpose the system maintains a *buffer* which keeps parts of tables in memory. Its contents changes frequently by reading from and writing to secondary storage whenever the database system has finished its operation on one part and needs buffer space for processing other parts. As read and write operations are time consuming they often dominate the overall time spent for the evaluation of queries. Decreasing the number of read and write operations usually improves the overall query processing time.

Suppose that the size of the buffer allows one to store three ordered streams of the initial stream *str*. Let f1 be the combination of sum_by and merge. Furthermore, assume that the resulting stream by applying f1 has (approximately) the same length as the initial two input streams such that it still fits into the available buffer space. If the condition holds for the new stream when applying f1, the latter transformation turns out to be superior: The intermediate stream res always resides in memory and is immediately accessible as input for the next application of f1. In contrast, the iterative program created by the first transformation proceeds in rounds. In case of more than three streams, each new stream created in round i is written out to secondary storage before read again in round $i + 1$. More formally, if there are n initial streams which are processed by sum_by and merge the program generated by the former transformation initiates $2n - 1$ read and $n - 1$ write operations under the above assumptions. The program generated with the latter transformation is superior since it uses only n read operations.

The assumptions made above are realistic for the computation of aggregates. Often, the number of values which determine the partition into subsets is much smaller than the number of tuples in the relation. Consider the initial query introduced at the beginning of this chapter and assume that the EMP relation contains 1000 tuples describing employees in 50 different departments. If function *conv_str* returns a stream of 10 streams, it is quite likely that each of them contains at least one employee in each department. The initial sorting and application of sum_by yields several streams each containing a tuple for each department, thus satisfying the above condition. Information about attribute values could help us to decide which of the transformations to apply.

5.2.2 Functional Transformation

In the previous section our focus was the transformation of control structures. We applied the transformation to the specification of sum_by and sort_merge. In its final form the application of merge to two streams str1 and str2 is immediately followed by the aggregate function sum_by. This section investigates the integration of both functions exploiting their recursive definitions. Using the transformation techniques developed in Chapter 3 we derive a new function sum_merge whose recursive definition easily translates into an iterative program which performs merging and summation at the same time.

The transformation is structured similarly to the one presented in Chapter 3. We unfold both functions and simplify the initial expression using transformation system $(\mathcal{T}_P, \mathcal{R}_P)$. sum_by calls function sum, so both steps are repeated for merge and sum. Instead of folding we use *abstraction* as the third transformation step [BD77]. We introduce the new function sum_merge to replace subexpressions in the transformed expression. To apply abstraction successfully some user guidance and additional transformations are needed.

During the transformation we shall use the following two assumptions about str1 and str2. They are implied by the transformation of the previous section:

1. Both streams are strictly ordered on values of A:

   (first str) $\leq_A$ (first (rest str))

2. For each element in one stream there exists at most one element in the other stream with the same A value. This assumption follows from the first one.

We begin the transformation of (sum_by (merge str1 str2))[2] by first unfolding both functions and applying transformation $(\mathcal{T}_P, \mathcal{R}_P)$. From assumption 1 it follows that (sum (first str) (rest str)) = str thus leading to the expression, $\mathcal{E}_0$:

---

[2]Henceforth we omit the subscripts B and A on both functions for convenience.

```
(if (empty? str1) str2
    (if (empty? str2) str1
        (if (gr? (first str1) (first str2))
            (sum (first str2) (merge str1 (rest str2)))
            (if (eq? (first str1) (first str2))
                (sum (first str2) (merge str1 (rest str2)))
                (sum (first str1) (merge (rest str1) str2))))))
```

$\mathcal{E}_0$ contains three calls to sum together with merge; so we focus on the expression

$$\text{(sum ele (merge str1 str2))}$$

We transform this more general expression first before considering actual parameters for ele, str1 and str2. Transformation system $(\mathcal{T}_P, \mathcal{R}_P)$ derives the following expression, $\mathcal{E}_1$:

```
(sum ele (merge str1 str2)) =
(if (empty? str1)
    (if (empty? str2) (out ele str1)
        (if (eq? ele (first str2))
            (sum (add ele (first str2)) (rest str2))
            (out ele (sum (first str2) (rest str2)))))
    (if (empty? str2)
        (if (eq? ele (first str1))
            (sum (add ele (first str1)) (rest str1))
            (out ele (sum (first str1) (rest str1))))
        (if (gr? (first str1) (first str2))
            (if (eq? ele (first str2))
                (sum (add ele (first str2)) (merge str1 (rest str2)))
                (out ele (sum (first str2) (merge str1 (rest str2)))))
            (if (eq? (first str1) (first str2))
                (if (eq? ele (first str2))
                    (sum (add ele (first str2)) (merge str1 (rest str2)))
                    (out ele (sum (first str2) (merge str1 (rest str2)))))
                (if (eq? ele (first str1))
                    (sum (add ele (first str1)) (merge (rest str1) str2))
```

```
(out ele (sum (first str1)
          (merge (rest str1) str1)))))))))
```

Now, we consider particular parameters for **ele**, **str1** and **str2** which are substituted into expression $\mathcal{E}_1$. We simplify $\mathcal{E}_1$ by taking advantage of additional conditions derived from calling environment of function sum in $\mathcal{E}_0$. According to the three calls we obtain three expressions $\mathcal{E}_2$, $\mathcal{E}_3$, and $\mathcal{E}_4$.

1. Consider the call (sum (first str1) (merge (rest str1) str2)):
   Conditions:

   - (gr (first str1) (first str2)) $\longrightarrow$ *false*

   - (empty? str2) $\longrightarrow$ *false*

   - (sum (first str2) (rest str2)) $\longrightarrow$ str2

   Applying these conditions to expression $\mathcal{E}_1$ we obtain expression $\mathcal{E}_2$:

```
(if (empty? (rest str1))
    (out (first str1) str2)
    (if (gr? (first (rest str1)) (first str2))
        (out (first str1)
             (sum (first str2) (merge (rest str1) (rest str2))))
        (out (first str1)
             (sum (first (rest str1)) (merge (rest (rest str1)) str2))
```

2. Consider the call (sum (first str2) (merge str1 (rest str2))):
   Conditions:

   - (gr (first str1) (first str2)) $\longrightarrow$ *true*

   - (empty? str1) $\longrightarrow$ *false*

   - (sum (first str1) (rest str1)) $\longrightarrow$ str1

   If we apply these conditions to expression $\mathcal{E}_1$ we obtain expression $\mathcal{E}_3$:

```
(if (empty? (rest str2))
    (out (first str2) str1)
    (if (gr? (first str1) (first (rest str2)))
        (out (first str2)
            (sum (first (rest str2))
                (merge str1  (rest (rest str2)))))
        (if (eq? (first str1) (first (rest str2)))
            (out (first str2)
                (sum (first (rest str2))
                    (merge str1 (rest (rest str2)))))
            (out (first str2)
                (sum (first str1)
                    (merge (rest str1) (rest str2)))))))
```

3. Consider the call (sum (first str2) (merge str1 (rest str2))):
   Conditions:

   - (gr (first str1) (first str2)) $\longrightarrow$ *true*

   - (empty? str1) $\longrightarrow$ *false*

If we apply these conditions to expression $\mathcal{E}_1$ we obtain expression $\mathcal{E}_4$:

```
(if (empty? (rest str2))
    (sum (add (first str2) (first str1)) (rest str1))
    (sum (add (first str2) (first str1))
        (merge (rest str1) (rest str2))))
```

The last derivation leads to a fourth call to function sum and merge with new
parameters:

4. (sum (add (first str2) (first str1))
       (merge (rest str1) (rest str2)))
   Conditions:

   - (empty? (rest str2)) $\longrightarrow$ *false*

Applying the condition to expression $\mathcal{E}_1$ we obtain expression $\mathcal{E}_5$:

```
(if (empty? (rest str2))
    (out (add (first str1) (first str2)) (rest str2))
    (if (gr? (first (rest str1)) (first (rest str2)))
        (out (add (first str2) (first str1))
            (sum (first (rest str2))
                (merge (rest str1) (rest (rest str2)))))
        (if (eq? (first (rest str1)) (first (rest str2)))
            (out (add (first str2) (first str1))
                (sum (first (rest str2))
                    (merge (rest str1) (rest (rest str2)))))
            (out (add (first str2) (first str1))
                (sum (first (rest str1))
                    (merge (rest (rest str1)) (rest str2)))))))
```

Additionally we transform

5. `(sum (add (first str2) (first str1)) (rest str2))`
   Conditions:

   - `(sum (first (rest str2))`

     `(rest (rest str2)))` $\longrightarrow$ `(rest str2)`

   - `(eq?  (add (first str2) (first str1))`

     `(first (rest str2)))` $\longrightarrow$ *false*

If we apply these conditions to expression $\mathcal{E}_1$ we obtain expression $\mathcal{E}_6$:

```
(out (add (first str2) (first str1)) (rest str2))
```

Note that $\mathcal{E}_5$ and $\mathcal{E}_6$ represent the transformed expressions for the two function calls in expression $\mathcal{E}_4$. We therefore continue the transformation by substituting expressions $\mathcal{E}_5$ and $\mathcal{E}_6$ for the two function subexpressions in $\mathcal{E}_4$. We also reverse the order of predicates (empty? str) using the rule

$$((if\ t_1\ t_2\ (if\ t_3\ t_2\ t_4)) \longrightarrow (if\ t_3\ t_2\ (if\ t_1\ t_2\ t_4)))$$

and use the equality (rest str1) = (rest str2) if both expressions are the empty stream. We obtain expression $\mathcal{E}_7$:

```
(if (empty? (rest str1))
    (out (add (first str2) (first str1)) (rest str2))
    (if (empty? (rest str2))
        (out (add (first str2) (first str1)) (rest str1))
        (if (gr? (first (rest str1)) (first (rest str2)))
            (out (add (first str2) (first str1))
                (sum (first (rest str2))
                    (merge (rest str1) (rest (rest str2)))))
            (if (eq? (first (rest str1)) (first (rest str2)))
                (out (add (first str2) (first str1))
                    (sum (first (rest str2))
                        (merge (rest str1) (rest (rest str2)))))
                (out (add (first str2) (first str1))
                    (sum (first (rest str1))
                        (merge (rest (rest str1)) (rest str2)))))))))
```

Expressions $\mathcal{E}_2$, $\mathcal{E}_3$, and $\mathcal{E}_7$ are the final output of the simplification step. For the third transformation step, *abstraction*, we introduce the new function (sum_merge str1 str2). The reader may have noticed the similarity between expressions $\mathcal{E}_2$, $\mathcal{E}_3$ and $\mathcal{E}_7$ and expression $\mathcal{E}_0$. We define the new function in terms of functions sum and merge:

```
(sum_merge str1 str2) =
(if (empty? str1) str2
    (if (empty? str2) str1
        (if (gr? (first str1) (first str2))
            (sum (first str2) (merge str1 (rest str2)))
            (if (eq? (first str1) (first str2))
                (sum (first str2) (merge str1 (rest str2)))
                (sum (first str1) (merge (rest str1) str2)))))))
```

If we apply the conditions for expression $\mathcal{E}_2$ to the body of **sum_merge** and distribute the function out with (first str1) as its first argument over the resulting expression both expressions are *identical*. Expression $\mathcal{E}_2$ therefore abstracts to

```
(out (first str1) (sum_merge (rest str1) str2))
```

Similarly, expression $\mathcal{E}_3$ is abstracted to

```
(out (first str2) (sum_merge str1 (rest str2))
```

Expression $\mathcal{E}_7$ yields the abstraction

```
(out (add (first str2) (first str1))
     (sum_merge str1 (rest str2)))
```

Substituting these abstractions into the initial definition of sum_merge for the corresponding calls to sum and merge we derive the new definition

```
(sum_merge str1 str2) =
(if (empty? str1) str2
    (if (empty? str2) str1
        (if (gr? (first str1) (first str2))
            (out (first str2) (sum_merge str1 (rest str2)))
            (if (eq? (first str1) (first str2))
                (out (add (first str2) (first str1))
                     (sum_merge str1 (rest str2)))
                (out (first str1) (sum_merge (rest str1) str2))))))
```

The new definition of sum_merge represents our final transformation result. We notice that the final definition has a *linear recursive form* which is the major achievement of the long derivation. Only this form enables us to produce an iterative program using a translation schema in [DB76].

5.3 Generalization of Transformation

The elaborate transformation on the functional level for aggregate functions leads to the natural question if the functional combination has to be repeated each time an aggregate function is combined with merge. An analysis of the transformation

100

shows that only the *structure* of both functions determines the translation. None of the translation steps depends on the the function add and sum. In fact, we could define more general functions **agg_by** and **agg** with

```
(agg_by f1 str) = (if (empty? str) *empty*
                       (agg f1 (first str) (rest str)))


(agg f1 ele str) =
    (if (empty str) (out ele str)
        (if (eq? ele (first str))
            (agg f1 (f1 ele (first str)) (rest str))
            (out ele (agg f1 (first str) (rest str)))))
```

f1 is a basic function which produces a new tuple from two tuples as its input. For our example, **f1** is equal to **add**, thus defining

$$(\text{sum\_by str}) = (\text{agg\_by add str})$$

The final transformation result of the previous section defines the new function (**agg_merge f1 str1 str2**) to be:

```
(agg_merge f1 str1 str2) =
(if (empty? str1) str2
    (if (empty? str2) str1
        (if (gr? (first str1) (first str2))
            (out (first str2) (agg_merge f1 str1 (rest str2)))
            (if (eq? (first str1) (first str2))
                (out (f1 (first str2) (first str1))
                    (agg_merge f1 str1 (rest str2)))
                (out (first str1) (agg_merge f1 (rest str1) str2)))))))
```

Using these definitions we may redefine other aggregate functions. For instance, the aggregate functions

$$(min\_by_{B,A} \; str) = \{t : \forall \, t' \in str : t'.A = t.A \implies t.B \leq_B t'.B\}$$
$$(max\_by_{B,A} \; str) = \{t : \forall \, t' \in str : t'.A = t.A \implies t.B \geq_B t'.B\}$$

are implemented by $(agg\_by_A\ min_B\ str)$ and $(agg\_by_A\ max_B\ str)$ with functions min_B and max_B returning the tuple with the smaller and larger values in attribute B, respectively. Similarly, the aggregate function

$$(count_A\ str) = \{t : t.CNT = |\ \{t' \in str : t'.A = t.A\}\ |\}$$

is implemented by $(sum\_by_{CNT,A}\ str')$ with each element of stream str extended by a new field CNT whose initial value is 1. Duplicate elimination is implemented by $(agg\_by_A\ one\ str)$ with function $(one\ t_1\ t_2)$ returning either tuple. The aggregate function $average$ with

$$(average\_by_{B,A}\ str) = \{t : t.AVG = \frac{\sum\{t_i.B : t_i \in str \wedge t_i.A = t.A\}}{|\ \{t_i \in str : t_i.A = t.A\}\ |}\}$$

needs some more attention. We notice that its computation is based on counting and summation. Using the notation $\ll\gg$ for horizontal loop fusion we define $(average\_by_{B,A}\ str) =$

$$(map*\ div_{B,CNT} \ll (sum\_by_{B,A}\ str)\ (count\_by_{CNT,A}\ str) \gg)$$

where div divides its first operand by its second.[3] The function $map*$ provides function div with its arguments by successively taking elements from both streams in "parallel". As for $map*$, we introduce the transformation rule

$$(\ll (agg\_by_A\ f_1\ str)(agg\_by_A\ f_2\ str) \gg \longrightarrow (agg\_by_A \ll f_1\ f_2 \gg\ str))$$

Replacing the functions sum_by and $count\_by$ by their corresponding definitions and applying the new rule, the example yields the expression

$$(agg\_by_A \ll add_B\ add_{CNT} \gg\ str')$$

$\ll add_B\ add_{CNT} \gg$ may be replaced by a new function

$$(add\_both_{B,CNT}\ t_1\ t_2) =<\ t_1.B + t_2.B,\ t_1.CNT + t_2.CNT,\ C>$$

for tuples $t_i =<\ B,\ CNT,\ C>$ with attributes B, CNT and C.

---

[3] A complete specification requires a more detailed description how the tuple format is changed by div; however for the current level of the transformation this is unimportant.

Using the results derived so far in this chapter we define a set of rewriting rules $\mathcal{R}_A$ which describes the transformations on aggregate functions and the sort-merge. $\mathcal{R}_A$ consists of the following rules:

$$\mathcal{R}_A = \{ \ (\ll (agg\_by_A \ f_1 \ str) \ (agg\_by_A \ f_2 \ str) \gg \longrightarrow (agg\_by_A \ \ll f_1 \ f_2 \gg \ str)),$$
$$((f_1 \ (tree \ f_2 \ str)) \xrightarrow{C} (tree \ (L \ f_1 \ f_2) \ (map* \ f_1 \ str))),$$
$$((L \ (agg\_by_A \ f_1) \ merge_A) \longrightarrow (agg\_merge_A \ f_1))\}$$

where condition C restricts the application of the rule to those functions with $(f_1 \ (f_2 \ str_1 \ str_2)) = (f_1 \ (f_2 \ (f_1 \ str_1) \ (f_1 \ str_2)))$.

The first rule implements horizontal loop fusion for the control structure agg_by_A. The second rule reflects the result of Theorem 5.2. The soundness of the last rule is based on the derivation of the previous section. Unfortunately, $\mathcal{R}_A$ cannot easily be extended by other rules to form a confluent term rewriting system. To obtain the desired transformation result, the rules are applied exhaustively in the order given. We demonstrate their application using the query:

Compute the variance in salary for each department

on the EMP relation introduced at the beginning of this chapter. Formally, we define the variance function

$$(var\_by_{Sal,Dept} \ str) = \{t : \ t.var = \mathcal{V}(\{t_i.Sal : \ t_i \in \text{EMP} \ \wedge \ (t_i.Dept = t.Dept) \})\}$$

with

$$\mathcal{V}(S) = 1/n \ * \ \sum_{i=1}^{n}(X_S - x_i) \ , \ \ X_S = 1/n \ * \ \sum_{i=1}^{n} x_i \ , \ \ n = |S| \ , \ x_i \in S$$

The definition of the variance suggests a two step computation: determine the average before the value for $\mathcal{V}(S)$ is computed. However, a simple manipulation of the initial definition yields

$$\mathcal{V}(S) = 1/n \ * \ \sum_{i=1}^{n} x_i^2 \ - \ 1/n^2 \ * \ (\sum_{i=1}^{n} x_i)^2$$

Using this definition for $\mathcal{V}(S)$, S has to be scanned only once to obtain its size, the sum of its elements, and the sum of the square values of its elements before function

$$(F_V \; CNT \; SUM \; SQR) = SQR/CNT - (SUM/CNT)^2$$

computes the final result. Using the definition for $\mathcal{V}(S)$ we define
$(var\_by_{Sal,Dept} \; str) =$

$$(map* \; F_V \ll\ll (count\_by_{Dept} \; str) \;\; (sum\_by_{Sal,Dept} \; str) \gg$$
$$(sqr\_by_{Sal,Dept} \; str) \gg)$$

where

$$sum\_by_{Sal,Dept} \;\; = \;\; (agg\_by_{Dept} \; add_{Sal} \; str')$$
$$count\_by_{Sal,Dept} \;\; = \;\; (agg\_by_{Dept} \; add_{CNT} \; str')$$
$$sqr\_by_{Sal,Dept} \;\; = \;\; (agg\_by_{Dept} \; add_{SQR} \; str')$$

and str' is obtained from str by adding two new fields CNT and SQR to all elements in str. These fields are initialized to 1 and the square of the salary, respectively. After substituting the definitions for all three aggregate functions, the first rule in $\mathcal{R}_A$ is applied twice. As the relation EMP must be sorted, the combination of the sort-merge and the aggregate definition yields the expression

$$(map* \; F_V \; (tree \; agm \; (map* \; agg \; (map* \; sort \; (conv\_str \; \text{EMP})))))$$

where

$$agm \;\; = \;\; (agg\_merge_{Dept} \ll\ll add_{Sal} \; add_{CNT} \gg add_{SQR} \gg)$$
$$agg \;\; = \;\; (agg\_by_{Dept} \ll\ll add_{Sal} \; add_{CNT} \gg add_{SQR} \gg)$$

using the second and third rule of $\mathcal{R}_A$. The transformation could be continued by using the first rule of $(\mathcal{T}_{map}, \mathcal{R}_{map})$ before proceeding with the manipulation of $(L \; agg \; sort)$. The final step transforms the high level specification into an iterative program using the translation schemes of Sections 5.2.1 and 3.4.

The example demonstrates the power of high level transformation. We exactly achieve the kind of optimization suggested by Klug [Klu82]. While he added new functions to implement this optimization, the derived rules automatically generate the improved programs.

Chapter 6

The Implementation of Database Systems in T

Our interest goes beyond a theoretical solution to the translation problem of relational queries. This chapter briefly discusses implementation aspects for database systems. The notation used throughout the previous chapters suggests a Lisp-like language for the implementation of our transformation algorithm. Most database systems are written in traditional systems programming languages, such as Assembler, C or PL/M [IMS75] [SW*76] [A*76]. Those languages facilitate fast execution. However, they do not support and manipulate high level data-structures and operations making coding, testing, and maintaining these large systems difficult. For this reason we decided to experiment with the Lisp dialect T developed at Yale University as our implementation language [RAM83] [RA82]. T supports operations on high level-data structures, such as lists and trees, and allows lazy evaluation as well as the dynamic creation of new functions. These language constructs are characteristic of many Lisp dialects. They provide a flexible environment to elegantly implement complex algorithms, often with less effort than in other languages. Unfortunately, programs written in Lisp languages often execute very slowly. Existing compilers do not produce efficient code for systems which demand fast execution. T was designed, in part, to supplement the interpreted programming environment with a compiler which generates efficient code. The combination of interpreter and compiler was intended to demonstrate that a language of highly expressive power is competitive in execution speed with traditional programming languages [RA82]. This claim encouraged us to implement

105

an *access method system*, a PDBP for database systems, using T. We also implemented an equivalent system in C. The implementation of an access method system combines several aspects of systems programming: manipulation of bits and bytes, access to functions of the underlying operating system and frequent need for type conversion. In the first section we investigate if T meets these requirements for such operations and how well those operations are integrated into the language. The second section discusses a performance comparison of both access method systems. The measurements show that the T implementation of the access method system is about twenty times slower than the corresponding C implementation. Although we do not expect T to perform as well as C, the high expressiveness of T cannot compensate for such a significant loss in execution speed in applications where performance is a critical parameter. The comparison indicates that T must address this performance problem to become a valuable tool for systems programming.

6.1   The Access Method System in T

To test T's applicability for systems programming we implemented an access method system for database systems in this language. The system consists of three levels. The lowest level implements the machine dependent functions to access the file system of the underlying operating system. They create, open, close, and destroy files, and read and write blocks of fixed size. The buffer manager on the second level insures that blocks are available in its buffers on request by higher level functions. If a requested block is not found in one of its buffers, the buffer manager finds a free buffer slot and then calls low-level functions to retrieve the block from secondary memory. The top level consists of a set of functions which create, destroy, open, and close relations and indices, and insert, retrieve, and delete tuples from relations or indices. We implemented our index-structure as B-trees.

For the successful implementation of all three levels we had to extend the functionality of the T language. The current T system does not support blocked file access. To overcome this deficiency we carefully examined T's source code for possible solutions. T provides a general interface to call functions of

106

the operating system for internal use. We call functions of the same interface to implement the file operations on the lowest level of our system. Once we discovered this interface we also used it to introduce other operating system services into T's implementation environment. In our opinion, T should provide a *general interface* which allows the programmer to use existing operating system services.

Our implementation of the access method system made apparent the need for functions to perform explicit type conversion. Tuples consist of fields containing values of different types, such as integers, reals or characters. Within the access method system they are mostly treated as strings of fixed length. Functions access substrings to retrieve field values according to some specified type. T does not provide functions to convert or interpret string values as values of other types. Again, T's source code helped us to find a solution to the problem. The system permits embedded functions written in *assembler language*. Those functions circumvent any type checking at execution time. Using T's ability to include assembler routines we implemented functions to convert integers and reals into strings and *vice versa*.

Our solution has major disadvantages. First, the assembler functions are written for a particular machine environment, making our code machine dependent. Second, their implementation relies on the knowledge of how type information is represented inside T. If this representation changes, these functions have to be rewritten. The question arises if these functions are necessary or if other tuple representations could avoid our problem. The representation of tuples as strings, i.e. as an "uninterpreted object", seems to be adequate as long as no field values are accessed. Strings are efficiently represented in secondary memory and delay interpretation and manipulation of tuples until necessary. Other forms of tuple representation — for instance as a list of fields, which is more consonant with the "Lisp philosophy" — prove to be unsatisfactory in performance. In those representations the conversion problem of tuples from their external to their internal form is done by the T system independent of its necessity.

We feel that a systems programming environment should permit the manipulation of data in any form. If necessary, the programmer should have the freedom to access data in a non-standard way and escape restrictions, usually imposed by the language. We suggest that T includes functions implementing type conversion.

Another solution to the problem is to provide facilities to include functions written in other languages into T's runtime environment. This solution provides a general mechanism to escape constraints imposed by T. T uses this ability for its own implementation. Other users of T have implemented functions to include programs written in C [Pat85].

Finally, we suggest that T needs to generate more efficient machine code. Without type information, extensive optimization is impossible. The next section will discuss T's unsatisfactory execution speed. A study of T's generated code shows that much overhead is produced by function calls to T internal or user-provided functions. Partial information about the actual parameters — for example type information — could reduce runtime overhead.

Consider the following example: the compiler translates the expression $(+\ a\ b)$ into a call to T's internal function which properly handles the addition of two numbers at runtime according to the type of the actual parameters. If a and b are known to be integers the expression could be replaced by $(fx+\ a\ b)$, where $fx+$ is *typed addition*. For typed addition, the compiler generates *one assembler instruction* instead of a function call. The dramatic difference in execution time shown by the results of the next section demonstrates the importance of type information. We suggest that T provides means to include such information in ways other than by textual changes of functions. Additional language facilities could help to systematically refine and tune programs by adding such information gradually when performance becomes an important aspect.

A more general approach for improving the performance of programs is promised by program transformation in the form of *partial evaluation* [B*76]. Partial evaluation takes a function f_1 of n arguments together with a list of i values for the first i arguments of f_1 and produces a new function f' with $n - i$ arguments, such that

$$(f'\ t_1 \ldots t_{n-i}) = (f_1\ c_1 \ldots c_i\ t_1 \ldots t_{n-i})$$

The specified values $c_1, \ldots, c_i$ may be numerical constants, functions, or other "fixed values", such as type information. Using the above example the addition could be expressed as ((*add type*) *a b*) where (*add type*) returns the proper addition function according to the available type information. If the type is *unknown* at compile time, the expression partially evaluates to (+ *a b*) and the compiler generates the appropriate call to T's internal add function. If the type is specified as *integer*, the partial evaluation yields the expression (*fx* + *a b*) and the compiler then generates one assembler instruction.

As an initial effort to support partial evaluation, T provides language facilities for inline expansion of functions into others at compile time. Its goal is to decrease the overhead of function calls. However, if functions are integrated over many levels, the size of the code produced by the compiler increases dramatically which may cause increased paging activities of the T system at runtime. A study of the produced code shows that the compiler rarely takes advantage of expanded functions to perform partial evaluation, even in cases where this task seems to be trivial. For example, the compiler evaluates the expression (*fx* + 2 3) to 5 while the corresponding untyped expression (+ 2 3) is left unevaluated.

T clearly needs improved code generation. Partial evaluation may be one way to achieve this goal. Although this task may not be always tractable, there exist many cases justifying partial evaluation as a valuable tool for optimization [B*76]. It may be desirable to let the user decide the extent of partial evaluation performed by the compiler. In the testing of programs there is little concern for performance; but when testing is completed and performance becomes an important aspect, the compiler should produce efficient code by optimization techniques such as partial evaluation.

6.2 Comparison of Access Methods

To obtain more quantitative results of T's execution speed, we implemented identical access method systems in T and C. We feel that the implementation of the access method systems can determine more accurately the performance trade-offs between both languages. We used object module size[1] to compare the quality of the code generated and to estimate the amount of overhead involved

---

[1]In our context a module describes a set of functions defined in one file.

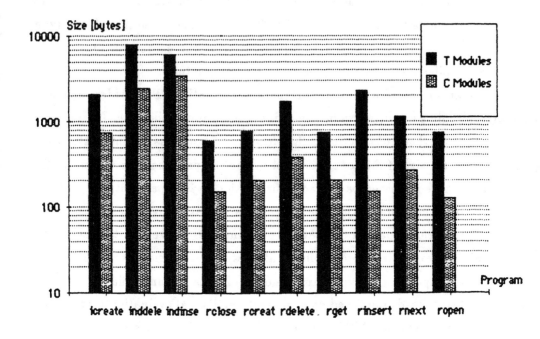

Figure 6.1: Program Size of Access Method Functions (Logarithmic Scale)

in the integration of compiled functions into T's runtime environment. We also measured the execution time of the different access method functions in C and T.

To compare the size of T and C modules we looked at functions implementing the third level of the access method system. We compiled all T functions without using inline expansion. The UNIX utility $size^2$ was used to determine the size of the executable and data segments of modules. We restricted our comparison to the executable part as a reasonable standard; we removed those parts from the executable segment containing string information about functions defined in this module. The chart of figure 6.2 shows the results of our measure-

---

[2]See UNIX programmer's manual 4.2 $size(1)$.

ments. The table in Appendix A.4 gives the exact values measured by function *size*.

The produced assembler code reveals some reasons why the T code is about four times larger than the corresponding C code:

1. *overhead for runtime integration* : much code is necessary to integrate compiled functions into T's runtime environment. This overhead is significant compared to the code which actually performs any computation.

2. *overhead in function calls* : All T functions contain many more function calls than the corresponding C functions.

3. *Overhead in string operations* : Many functions in the access method system involve extensive string manipulation. While C performs string operations by using pointers the corresponding manipulation in T always requires calls to T's internal string manipulation functions.

The second comparison of T and C functions is based on their execution time. We implemented two functions using the UNIX system call *vtimes*[3] to measure time in both environments. T provides several ways to change the execution speed of functions. We already mentioned compilation and inline expansion as two important options. To estimate the benefit of the latter we compiled the access method system twice: once by taking advantage of inline expansion and once without this option. We surprisingly discovered that inline expansion had little effect on the execution speed; no considerable difference was measured. We could not find any satisfying or convincing argument to explain our results. Possibly the remaining function calls still dominate the execution time. It seems unlikely that the increased module size of the expanded version dramatically influenced the paging activities for T. We decided not to investigate this aspect further. In the sequel all measurements refer to compilations without inline expansion unless otherwise noted.

---

[3] see UNIX Programmer's Manual 4.2 *vtimes*(3C).

Another important factor is the amount of runtime checking. T allows the user to decide on the extent of runtime checking. Less checking implies faster execution. We distinguish between *minimal* and *extensive* runtime checking.[4]

Before discussing the execution time of the access method functions, we present the time measurements for another set of functions. We wrote eight T functions, called *s1* to *s8*, which independently test particular language facilities used frequently in our implementation. The code is provided in Appendix A.2. A loop executes the same operations several times to obtain reliable results. The comparison of *s1/s2*, *s3/s4*, and *s1/s5* shows the impact of *typed operations* on the execution speed. We estimate time for *function calls* by comparing *s1* and *s6*. *s7* and *s8* compare the two string functions *string_slice* and *substring*.[5] The former provides access to a substring within a string; the latter returns a copy of the specified substring. When possible we also implemented the corresponding C functions which are listed in Appendix A.3.

Figure 6.2 graphically shows the measured results for all eight functions. Appendix A.5 shows the measurements in tabular form. The chart displays the execution time for interpreted code and compiled code using extensive and minimal runtime checking. The compiled functions execute two to four times faster than the interpreted versions. Minimal runtime checking contributes another factor of two. With one exception, the fastest execution of each function is still *fifty times slower* than the execution of the corresponding C function. The exception is function *s2* which runs compiled almost as fast as the equivalent C function. The result is no surprise. The discussion in the previous section revealed that the compiler generates *one assembler statement* for the typed addition instead of a function call, thus making its execution competitive with the C function. Similarly, *s3* and *s4* show the improvement for typed comparisons; but the two untyped operations continue to dominate the overall execution time since they are compiled into function calls. Our observation suggests that T must improve the speed of function calls to guarantee faster execution. Our claim is supported by the comparison of *s1* and *s5*. They show that a call may take as long as

---

[4]See *T Manual*: recklessness.

[5]See *T Manual*: string operations

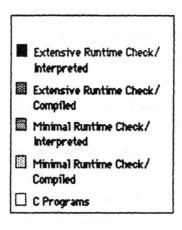

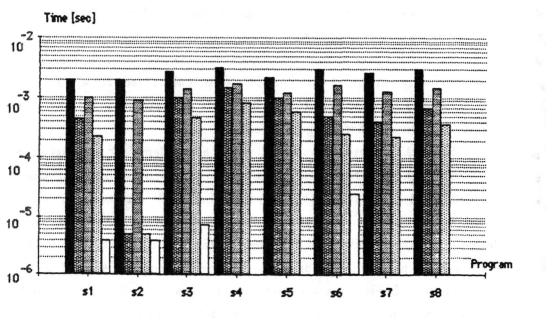

Figure 6.2: Runtime of Simple Functions (Logarithmic Scale)

113

0.5 *msec* while the corresponding time in C is at least ten times faster. Finally, the results for $s7$ and $s8$ suggest using the function *string_slice* rather than function *substring*. Creating a pointer into an existing string is less time consuming than copying a substring into a new location.

Using the same standards as for $s1$ to $s8$, we evaluated the different access method functions. Figure 6.3 displays the results graphically. Appendix A.6 shows the measurements in tabular form. Again, the compiled functions run about twice as fast as the interpreted ones. Reduced runtime checking improves the execution speed by another factor of two. The corresponding C functions are still about *twenty* times faster than the T functions. In addition to the reasons given before, there are two more important reasons for the significant time difference. First, strings and substrings in C are accessed by pointers. The corresponding operations in T always require a function call which performs the string access via an internally defined string header. The internal representation creates considerable overhead for these operations. Second, the type conversion functions which we discussed in the previous section also contribute significantly to the execution time in T. In C only negligible overhead exists for any type conversion between strings, integers or reals.

The overall analysis shows why T suffers a considerable loss in execution speed. Although we did not expect T to perform as well as C, the difference by a factor of twenty exceeds the acceptable limits. We outlined suggestions how to overcome the described problems to improve T's implementation. With additional language facilities and improved compilation, T could become a competitive systems programming language as far as performance is concerned. Much of the power of other systems programming languages comes from their flexibility in handling type conversion. A more detailed investigation is necessary to integrate type conversion in T.

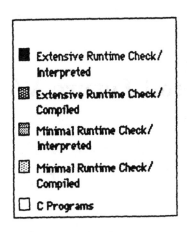

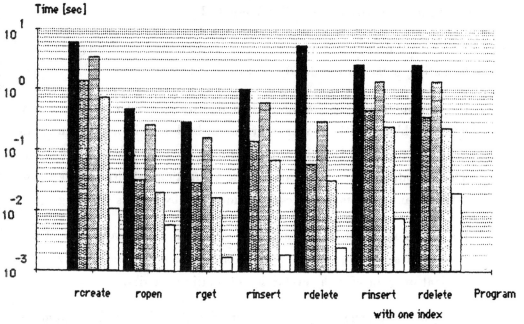

Figure 6.3: Runtime of Access Method Functions (Logarithmic Scale)

Chapter 7

Conclusion and Future Work

We see the major contributions of this thesis to be

1. the successful application of functional programming and program transformation in the area of database systems.

2. the development of two transformation algorithms to solve the query translation problem. Without user intervention both algorithms systematically generate structured iterative programs from modular query specifications. The first algorithm is based on recursive function definitions; the second takes advantage of map expressions motivated by Backus' FP language.

3. the extension of the transformational approach to the translation of multiple queries. We apply the technique of horizontal loop fusion to generate efficient programs for the evaluation of multiple queries.

4. the systematic generation of more efficient algorithms and programs for the evaluation of aggregate functions in relational database systems. We demonstrate how to generate iterative programs from independent specifications for sorting and aggregation. The transformation combines different techniques of program transformation.

5. the combination of low and high level transformation. For the transformation of aggregate functions we prove the soundness of a transformation rule for map expressions by a lengthy, user guided transformation using recursive function definitions.

6. the definition and derivation of new control structure operators for programs evaluating aggregate functions. The operators *agg_by* and *merge_by* are introduced during the transformation process.

7. the performance study of the Lisp dialect T as an alternative implementation language for database systems. T with its high expressiveness provides the necessary data structures and operations which simplify the implementation of complex systems. If performance is relevant factor, T's current execution speed is not satisfactory. We discuss several reasons for its slow execution speed and outline suggestions how to improve T as a systems programming language.

The results of this thesis demonstrate that ideas and techniques of functional programming and program transformation help to solve problems in the area of database systems. Although the results are encouraging, more evidence is necessary to show that the approach taken in this thesis is powerful enough to solve other problems for database systems as well. We suggest investigating the following problems:

1. A more complete set of operators: We would like to include actions which create intermediate streams during their evaluation and non-algebraic actions.

2. Different tuple representations: Throughout this thesis we use "flat tuples", i.e. tuples which consist of fields with attribute values of basic types, such as integer, real, or string values. All operations on tuples assume this representation. However, certain evaluation strategies need more complex tuple structures. For example, Dayal introduces hierarchical tuples to evaluate quantified queries efficiently [Day83]. To include this evaluation strategy, we need to separate the structural representation of tuples from the operations performed on them. A transformation system should combine tuple operations with information about their representation to programs which guarantee efficient execution. This aspect becomes even more important with new requirements for more complex field types, such as relations [Lam84] or graphic types [WW76].

3. the application of the transformational approach to other problems of database systems. For example, Shasha describes general operations on data structures which include locking operations; the data structure itself is left unspecified [Sha84]. When a particular data structure is chosen, we would like to derive efficient operations for its manipulation using the transformational approach.

The work of [Sha84] leads to the more general question of how to support the modular design and implementation of database systems in general. Currently, the different components in most database systems are highly integrated which makes desirable changes almost impossible. A high level specification of the various components, like the user interface, the query optimizer, the access method system, the concurrency control component, or the logging and recovery component, could make changes easier. A powerful transformation system, possibly including some user guidance could help to generate database systems which meet the demands for high performance. For this purpose more work is necessary to better understand the interaction between different components in a database system.

Appendix

Measurements of T and C Functions

A.1 Test Configuration

Computer	: VAX780; 4Mb Memory
Operating System	: UNIX Berkeley 4.2
T Interpreter	: T 2.6
T Compiler	: TC 1.3

A.2 Simple T Functions

```
;;;
;;; simple loop without loop body
;;;
   (define (s1 n)
     (do ((i 1 (1+ i)))
         ((fx> i n) T)))


;;;
;;; as s1 but typed increment
;;;
   (define (s2 n)
     (do ((i 1 (fx+ 1 i)))
         ((fx> i n) T)))


;;;
;;; as s1 but with body
;;;
   (define (s3 n)
     (do ((i 1 (1+ i)) (j 0))
         ((fx> i n) T)
         (set j (1+ j)))))
```

```
;;;
;;; as s3 but untyped comparison
;;;
    (define (s4 n)
      (do ((i 1 (1+ i)) (j 0))
          ((> i n) T)
          (set j (1+ j))))


;;;
;;; as s1 but  untyped comparison
;;;
    (define (s5 n)
      (do ((i 1 (1+ i)))
          ((> i n) T)))


;;;
;;; functions call
;;;
    (define (s6 n)
      (do ((i 1 (1+ i)))
          ((fx> i n) T)
          (s6test i)))

    (define (s6test i)
      (fx+ i i))
```

```
;;;
;;;   testing string-slice
;;;
   (define (s7 n)
     (do ((i 1 (fx+ 1 i)))
         ((fx> i n) T)
         (string-slice teststring i 10 )))


;;;
;;; testing substring
;;;
   (define (s8 n)
     (do ((i 1 (fx+ 1 i)))
         ((fx> i n) T)
         (substring teststring i 10 )))
```

A.3   Simple C Functions

```
/*          loop without body                */

s1 (n) int n;
   { int i; for (i=0; i<=n; i++); }



/*          loop with body                    */

s3 (n) int n;
    { int i, j; for (i=0; i<=n; i++) j = j+1; }



/*          loop with function call           */

s6 (n) int n;
    { int i; for (i=0; i<=n; i++) s6test(i); }

s6test (i) int i; { i++; }
```

A.4 Program Size of Access Method Functions

The size of a program is measure in bytes. The results were obtained executing the *size* command in UNIX. The size of the executable (.text) part is used.

Size Measured in Bytes			
Function	T Version	T Version*	C Version*
icreate	2760	2080	740
inddelete	8848	7840	2488
indinsert	7168	6048	3400
close	816	592	152
rcreate	1080	768	204
rdelete	2264	1696	376
rget	968	736	204
rinsert	3040	2264	152
rnext	1440	1160	264
ropen	1048	752	128

* The result of this column was obtained by removing a major part of the executable program segment which only contains strings naming calling and called functions

Table A.1: Program Size of Access Method Functions

A.5 Runtime of Simple Functions

	Time Measured for Simple Functions				
	Extensive Runtime Check		Minimal Runtime Check		
Function	Interpreted*	Compiled*	Interpreted*	Compiled*	C Version*
	10^{-3}	10^{-4}	10^{-3}	10^{-4}	10^{-6}
S1	2	4.5	1	2.3	4
S2	2	0.05	0.9	0.05	4
S3	2.8	10	1.4	4.7	7.5
S4	3.2	15	1.7	8.3	
S5	2.2	10	1.2	6	
S6	3	5	1.6	2.5	25
S7	2.7	4	1.3	2.3	
S8	3	7	1.5	3.6	

* Column has to be multiplied by the factor provided in the next row to obtain time in seconds

Table A.2: Runtime of Simple Functions

A.6 Runtime of Access Method Functions

Time Measured for Access Method Functions					
	Extensive Runtime Check		Minimal Runtime Check		
Function	Interpreted*	Compiled*	Interpreted*	Compiled*	C Version*
	1	10^{-1}	1	10^{-2}	10^{-3}
rcreate	5.9	13	3.3	70	11
ropen	0.47	0.33	0.25	2	6
rinsert**	1.0	1.4	0.6	7	2
rdelete**	0.54	0.6	0.3	3.3	2.6
rinsert***	2.5	4.5	1.3	24	8
rdelete***	2.5	3.6	1.3	23	20

* Column has to be multiplied by the factor provided in the next row to obtain time in seconds; ** without index; *** with one index

Table A.3: Runtime of Access Method Functions

Bibliography

[A*76]   Astrahan et al. "SYSTEM R : Relational Approach to Database Management". *ACM Transactions on Database Systems Vol.1, No.2*, pages 97–137, June 1976.

[ASU72]   A. Aho, R. Sethi, and J.D Ullman. "Code Optimization and Finite Church-Rosser Systems". R. Rustin, editor, *Proceedings of Courant Computer Science Symposium 5*, pages 89–105, Prentice Hall, Englewood Cliffs, N.J., 1972.

[B*76]   Lennart Beckman et al. "A Partial Evaluator and its Use as a Programming Tool". *Artificial Intelligence 7*, pages 319–357, 1976.

[Bac78]   J. Backus. "Can Programming be Liberated from the von Neuman Style ? A Functional Style and its Algebra of Programs". *Communications of the ACM Vol.21, No.8*, pages 613–641, August 1978.

[BD77]   R.M. Burstall and J. Darlington. "A Transformation System for Developing Recursice Programs". *Journal of the ACM 24, No. 1*, pages 44–67, January 1977.

[BD83]   D. Bitton and D.J. DeWitt. "Duplicate Record Elimination in Large Data Files". *ACM Transactions on Database Systems Vol.8, No.2*, pages 255–265, June 1983.

[Bel84]   F. Bellegarde. "Rewriting Systems on FP Expressions that Reduce the Number of Sequences They Yield". *ACM Symposium on LISP and Functional Programming*, pages 63–73, Austin, Texas, August 1984.

[BF82]   Peter Buneman and Robert E. Frankel. "An Implementation Technique for Database Query Languages". *ACM Transactions on Database Systems Vol.7, No.2*, pages 164–186, June 1982.

[Bir84]   R.S. Bird. "The Promotion and Accumulation Strategies in Transformational Programming". *ACM Transactions on Programming Languages and Systems, Vol.6, No.4*, pages 487–504, October 1984.

[BMS80] R.M. Burstall, D.B. MacQueen, and D.T. Sannella. *"HOPE an Experimental Applicative Language"*. Technical Report, Department of Computer Science, University of Edinburgh, 1980.

[Cod70]   E.F. Codd. "A Relational Model of Data for Large Shared Data Banks". *Communications of the ACM Vol.13, No.6*, pages 377–387, June 1970.

[Coh80]   N.H. Cohen. *"Source-to-Source Improvement of Recursive Programs"*. PhD Thesis, Harvard University, May 1980.

[Col84]   L. Colussi. "Recursion as an Effective Step in Program Development". *ACM Transactions on Programming Languages and Systems Vol.6, No.1*, pages 55–67, January 1984.

[Day83]   U. Dayal. "Evaluating queries with quantifiers: a horticultural approach". *Proc. Symposium on Principles of Database Systems*, pages 125–136, Atlanta, March 1983.

[DB76]   J. Darlington and R.M. Burstall. "A System which Automatically Improves Programs". *Acta Informatica 6, No. 1*, pages 41–60, 1976.

[DM79]   N. Dershowitz and Z. Manna. "Proving Termination with Multiset Orderings". *Communications of the ACM Vol.22, No.8*, pages 465–476, August 1979.

[FW76]   D.P. Friedman and D.S. Wise. "CONS Should not Evaluate its Arguments". S. Michaelson and R.Milner, editors, *Automata, Languages, and Programming*, pages 257–284, Edinburgh University Press, Edinburgh, 1976.

[GK84]   J.S. Givler and R.B. Kieburtz. "Schema Recognition for Program Transformation". *ACM Symposium on LISP and Functional Programming*, pages 74–84, Austin, Texas, August 1984.

[GP84]   A. Goldberg and R. Paige. "Stream Processing". *ACM Symposium on LISP and Functional Programming*, pages 53–62, Austin, Texas, August 1984.

[HM76]   P. Henderson and J.H. Morris. "A Lazy Evaluator". *3rd ACM SIGACT-SIGPLAN Symposium on Principles of Programming Languages*, pages 96–103, Atlanta, 1976.

[Hue80] G. Huet. "Confluent Reductions: Abstract Properties and Applications of Term Rewriting Systems". *Journal of the ACM Vol.27, No.4*, pages 797–821, October 1980.

[IMS75] IMS:. *"Information Management System, General Information Manual"*. IBM Pub. No. GH20-1260, IBM Corp., White Plains, NY, 1975.

[JW75]   K. Jensen and N. Wirth. *"PASCAL User Manual and Report"*. Springer-Verlag, Berlin, Heidelberg, New York, 1975.

[KB70]   D.E. Knuth and P. Bendix. "Simple Word Problems in Universal Algebras". J. Leech, editor, *Computational Problems in Abstract Algebra*, pages 263–297, Pergamon Press, Elmsford, N.Y., 1970.

[Klu82] A. Klug. "Access Paths in the Abe Statistical Query Facility". *ACM Sigmod Conference on Mangement of Data*, pages 161–173, 1982.

[Knu73] D.E. Knuth. *"The Art of Computer Programming Vol.3"*. Addison-Wesley, Reading, MA, 1973.

[KR78]   B.W. Kernighan and D.R. Ritchie. *"The C Programming Language"*. Prentice-Hall, Inc., 1978.

[Lam84] W. Lamersdorf. "Recursive Data Models for Non-Conventional Database Applications". *Proc. Computer Data Engineering Conference, IEEE Computer Society*, pages 143–162, Los Angeles, April 1984.

[LB79]   R.A. Lorie and B.W. Wade. *"The Compilation of a High Level Data Language"*. Technical Report, IBM Research Laboratory, San Jose, CA 95193, 1979.

[Mey82] A. Meyer. "What is a Model of Lambda Calculus?". *Information and Control 52*, pages 87–122, 1982.

[MN70]   Z. Manna and S. Ness. "On the Termination of Markov Algorithms". *3rd Hawaii International Conference on System Science*, pages 789–892, January 1970.

[Pat85] D. Patel. Private communication with D. Patel (patel@ucla-locus.ARPA), 1985.

[RA82]   J.A. Rees and N.I. Adams. "T: A Dialect of LISP or, LAMBDA: The Ultimate Software Tool". *ACM Symposium on LISP and Functional Programming*, pages 114–122, August 1982.

[RAM83] J.A. Rees, N.I. Adams, and J.R. Meehan. *"The T Manual"*. Computer Science Department, Yale Unversity, New Haven, CT, 1983.

[Ros73] B.K. Rosen. "Tree Manipulating Systems and Church-Rosser Theorems". *Journal of the ACM Vol.20, No.1*, pages 160–187, January 1973.

[RR82]   A. Rosenthal and D. Reiner. "An Architecture for Query Optimization". *ACM-SIGMOD Conference on Management of Data*, pages 246–255, 1982.

[Sha84] D. Shasha. *"Concurrent Algorithms for Search Structures"*. PhD thesis, Harvard University, May 1984.

[Ste77] G.L. Steele. "Debunking the "Expensive Procedure Call" Myth or, Procedure Call Implementations Considered Harmful or, Lambda: The Ultimate Goto". *ACM National Conference*, pages 153–162, Washington, October 1977.

[Sto77] J.E. Stoy. *"Denotational Semantics"*. MIT Press, Cambridge, MA, 1977.

[SW*76] M. Stonebraker, E. Wong, et al. "The Design and Implementation of INGRES". *ACM Transactions on Database Systems Vol.1, No.3*, pages 189–222, September 1976.

[Ten76] R. Tennent. "The Denotational Semantics of Programming Languages". *Communications of the ACM Vol.19, No.8*, pages 437–453, August 1976.

[Tur80] D.A. Turner. "Programming Languages - Current and Future Developments". *Infotech State of the Art Conference on Software Development Techniques*, 1980.

[Ull82] J.D. Ullman. *"Principles of Database Systems"*. Computer Science Press, San Francisco, 1982.

[Wan80] M. Wand. "Continuation-Based Program Transformation Strategies". *Journal of the ACM Vol.27, No.1*, pages 164–180, January 1980.

[Wil82] J.H. Williams. "Notes on the FP Style of Functional Programming". J. Darlington, P. Henderson, and D.A. Turner, editors, *Functional Programming and its Applications*, pages 193–215, Cambridge University Press, 1982.

[WW76] D. Weller and R. Williams. "Graphic and Relational Data Base Support for Problem Solving". *3rd Annual Conference on Computer Graphics, Interactive Techniques and Image Processing, ACM SIGGRAPH Computer Graphics Vol.10, No.2*, pages 183–189, 1976.